Robert Forman Horton

The teaching of Jesus in eighteen sections

Robert Forman Horton

The teaching of Jesus in eighteen sections

ISBN/EAN: 9783337257729

Printed in Europe, USA, Canada, Australia, Japan

Cover: Foto ©Lupo / pixelio.de

More available books at **www.hansebooks.com**

THE
TEACHING OF JESUS

IN EIGHTEEN SECTIONS

BY

ROBERT F. HORTON

AUTHOR OF
"INSPIRATION AND THE BIBLE" "REVELATION AND THE BIBLE"
"THE CARTOONS OF ST. MARK" ETC

LONDON
ISBISTER AND COMPANY Limited
15 & 16 TAVISTOCK STREET COVENT GARDEN
1895

Printed by BALLANTYNE, HANSON & CO.
At the Ballantyne Press.

ECCLESIÆ NOSTRÆ
DE ME OPTIME MERITÆ
HÆC OPTIMA MEA
DEDICO

PREFACE

WHEN Wendt's exhaustive work, *Lehre Jesu*, appeared, it was evident that a new starting-point for theological reconstruction had been given to the world. It was a matter of regret that so magnificent a work should be marred by certain presuppositions which belong to the Ritschlian School. Beyschlag in his *New Testament Theology* offered some minor criticisms of Wendt's work, but did not unfortunately alter that defect, which was the most serious blot on the *Lehre Jesu*, the attempt to explain away one of the most indubitable elements of the teaching of Jesus, the fact of His pre-existence.

I felt it my duty to give to my own Church the main results of these two invaluable books, especially in the hope that I might remove the great defect, while passing on the splendid spoil which these scholars had carried away from the study of years.

I have now thrown the substance of eighteen sermons on the subject into the present form. The homiletic—though not the didactic—setting has been laid aside, in order to save time and space With the utmost conciseness I have endeavoured to sketch the teaching of Jesus as it has been presented to us by the labours of such authorities as Wendt and Beyschlag.

I cannot anticipate a large number of readers, for it is the unhappy delusion of the Church that it knows the teaching of Jesus. Possibly, if I were to give the book a true but sensational title, "The Revolution of Theology," the Church would pay attention to it. On the other hand, men of the world have small interest in the teaching of Jesus because they have not marked the distinction between it and the teaching of the Church. "Hear the Church" has been the cry of centuries. They have done so. "Hear Him" is, I would fain hope, the cry of this book.

ROBERT F. HORTON.

HAMPSTEAD, *September* 1895.

CONTENTS

	PAGE
INTRODUCTION: THE TEACHING OF JESUS . . .	11

PART I.—THE SYNOPTICS

THE KINGDOM	25
THE SON OF MAN	39
THE FATHER	53
SIN	67
RIGHTEOUSNESS	81
SALVATION	95
THE MEANS OF SALVATION	109
THE CHURCH	125
THE JUDGMENT	139

PART II.—ST. JOHN

THE CROWN OF THE TEACHING	155
THE NATURE OF THE FATHER	171
THE NATURE OF THE SON	187
THE PRE-EXISTENCE OF JESUS	203
ETERNAL LIFE	219
THE DEATH OF JESUS	235
THE COMMUNITY OF BELIEVERS	251
THE RESURRECTION	267

THE TEACHING OF JESUS

THERE is a new breath in modern theology, as if the air of spring were stealing from the stiff lips of winter, and the Christian faith were about to become again the animating spirit of men and nations. It is due to a remarkable revival of interest in the teaching of Jesus. The attraction of that subject is amazing. When Wendt's careful and exhaustive study appeared in an English form I chanced to refer to it in a sermon, and letter after letter came to me asking for particulars. I seemed to hear the earnest voice of England saying, Tell us what He taught.

Considering that His teaching is all contained within the narrow compass of the four Gospels, one would suppose that every one had some exhaustive acquaintance with it. "What need," you might ask, "for any book at all on the contents of the most familiar and the most limpidly clear of all English books? Surely every one knows and quotes the sayings of Christ?" Yes, but few know the teaching of Jesus. Few, even among theologians and preachers, have made a study of it.

I had occasion last year to read through the

works of that great Puritan divine, John Howe; and in six octavo volumes of treatises and discourses I found no allusion to the teaching of Jesus as such, the teaching as a whole, the teaching as the main authority in religion. Stranger still, quite recently Dr. Denney has published some brilliant and instructive lectures which he delivered at Chicago as an informal manual of orthodox theology.[1] In this stimulating volume all the problems of religion are handled. But there is no reference to the teaching of Jesus, except when the lecturer wishes to treat of the Church and the Last Judgment. He then refers to the reputed sayings of our Lord upon these subjects —almost the only subjects of His teaching on which our records are confused and uncertain.

But the strangest fact of all is that when we go back to the New Testament itself we find that the most voluminous of the apostolic writers, St. Paul, does not allude to the teaching except in the most casual way. Though the oral tradition which is embodied in our Gospels must have been current in the apostolic circles, and familiar to those first witnesses as the alphabet of religion, it does not appear to have formed the subject of their preaching. What is the explanation of this anomaly? It would seem that the wonder of the Cross, the Resurrection and the Ascension, obliterated in a blaze of glory every other consideration. "He died for our sins and rose again for our justification." "Himself

[1] I am delighted to see that this book has already run through several editions, and has been recognised as one of the great contributions to theology of the year 1895.

bore our sins in His own body on the tree." "He is the propitiation for our sins." The mind was filled and dazed with that triumph over sin and death, that entrance into heaven, and the door opened to all believers. The first apostles stood in adoring gratitude around an empty tomb, and gazed up into heaven where they saw Christ sitting at the right hand of God. Just as we think far less of the sermons, powerful and witty as they were, of Ridley, Hooper and Latimer, than of their heroic martyrdom; just as Savonarola the teacher is merged in Savonarola the sufferer; so, only in a still higher degree, Jesus, the prophet of Galilee, the lawgiver of the Sermon on the Mount, was almost forgotten in Christ the crucified one, Christ the risen one, Christ the returning judge.

Thus even from apostolic times the bias to which I refer has been observable in the Church. The teaching of Jesus has been neglected in favour of the central fact in His saving work. At times, and in many churches, the connection between the two has been lost. And it needs little argument to prove that Christianity, as we know it—as it has been known since the beginning of the second century—shows but slight and occasional traces of some things which figured largely in the teaching of its founder.

And yet the reiterated insistence, and the bulk, of the Gospel narrative in our New Testament, will never let us rest content with the omission. Before we can reach the first word of apostolic teaching about Jesus, we have to read a fourfold record of His teaching on religion and life, on the apostles themselves, and on the whole course of human affairs. We are not permitted to forget that in the first instance He appeared as a teacher. "They were all amazed, insomuch that they questioned among themselves, saying, What is this? A new teaching!"[1] "He taught them as one having authority."[2] Thus they thought He must be one of the ancient prophets *redivivus*.[3] And even in looking back upon His life at the moment of their bereavement, the main impression left upon their minds was that of "a prophet mighty in deed and word before God and all the people."[4]

He was of course quite explicit in saying that He was more than a prophet, nor is it possible for the Church to rest content with the recognition of Him as a teacher. His own teaching forbids such a limitation. The work which He had come to do, the work of which He said that He was straitened until it was accomplished, was obviously something greater and more arduous than simply the utterance of truth. But we cannot think that His teaching was only an incident. We cannot dismiss it as applicable only to that place and time—as a preparation, a scaffolding to pass away when the building should be reared. For He expressly said that His word should not pass away. And further, His saving work is so vitally connected with His teaching, both as a cause, a means, and an end, that if we lose sight of the teaching the doctrine of redemption

[1] Mark i. 27.
[2] Matt. vii. 29.
[3] Mark viii. 28; Matt. xvi. 14.
[4] Luke xxiv. 19.

itself ceases to convince the understanding and to grip the conscience.

It is the misfortune of the Church that she has always been tempted, following the lines of the Pauline epistles in a way which Paul himself never would have done, to construct a theory of atonement, of justification, sanctification and redemption, which is practically independent of her Lord's teaching. Thus she has often arrived at a view of salvation which does not include salvation from sin, and at an expectation of eternal life which has no connection with a Christ-like life on earth.

But whenever, even for a moment, she has got back to the teaching of her Lord, wonderful things have happened. An *Imitatio Christi* has been written for the lasting guidance of the devout, or a life of St. Francis has been lived, a sweet and powerful copy of the Lord's own life. And here in our day again men are struggling back to that potent teaching. Leo Tolstoi is stirring Europe by an honest, however one-sided, attempt to face and to frankly accept it. And in thousands of minds less eminent it is working like a seed, pushing through the dull dust of the ages, and already filming the dry branches of life with the green promise of spring.

I appeal, therefore, for your close and continuous attention to a brief exercise in the teaching of Jesus.

It would hardly do to pass to our study of the teaching without saying a word about the authority and the source from which it is derived. It is all contained in the four Gospels; but the Gospels have been so pitilessly criticised, and so vehemently assailed, that some careless observers have concluded that their authenticity has been discredited. I have not time for a detailed proof of the fact that modern inquiries have served rather to establish than to weaken the trustworthiness of these ancient records. But I will state in a sentence or two the kind of reasons which allow us to believe that we have here the genuine teaching of Jesus.

One clear fact may serve as the keystone of the external evidence, which Bishop Lightfoot has reared in the face of this generation, a noble and durable arch sufficient in itself to support the belief that our Gospels are genuine history, coming from the circle of the eye-witnesses of the events. The fact I select is this: Papias, whom Irenæus in the last quarter of the second century already speaks of as *an ancient* (ἀρχαῖος ἀνήρ), tells us how carefully he gathered from the first disciples and their followers the commandments which came from the Lord Himself. He was inclined to trust the living voice more than written records, and was therefore particular to converse with these apostolic men as he had opportunity. Here, then, is a contemporary of the evangelists, whose life falls between 70 and 150 A.D. And it is he who gives us our earliest notice of the Gospels. "Mark," he says, "who became the interpreter of Peter, accurately, though not in any particular order, wrote what he remembered of Christ's utterances and deeds. It was his one thought to omit nothing that he heard and to falsify nothing. Matthew compiled the *Logia* (which may mean the discourses, or possibly, as Dr. Charteris thinks, the general narrative of the life) in the Aramaic language, and every one rendered them as he could."

It would be difficult to have earlier or more direct testimony to the fact that our Gospel records come from Peter and Matthew, two of the first disciples. We have no such evidence for the poems of Homer or the histories of Tacitus. With such evidence, of which the fact I have stated is only an item, no one would ever have questioned the antiquity and the authenticity of the teaching, but that the contents of the Gospels necessarily pass a judgment upon us all, and every Christless man is naturally eager to disprove Christ.

The difficulty some have felt in realising how the words of Jesus could be retained in the memory of those that heard until they were committed to writing need not detain us. His sayings are of that pithy and picturesque character that easily makes a lasting impression on the memory, and it is evident that He took particular pains to fix His teaching in the minds of the choosen few,[1] so that, until they were capable of grasping His meaning, they should at least be secure of the words.

I may also, in passing, call your attention to a curious little mark of the antiquity and authenticity of the first three Gospels. In all three we find on the lips of Jesus the saying that *this generation* (αὐτὴ γενέα) *shall not pass away until all these things be*

---
[1] Mark iv. 10-32.

accomplished.[1] "These things" include not only the events of the destruction of Jerusalem, but also the signs and wonders of the last day. Not only that generation, but fifty generations more have passed and yet all "these things" are not fulfilled. Now, as we shall see, this apparent falsification of a prophecy is probably due to a confusion in the records of two very distinct discourses. But how absolutely incredible it is that the confusion should have occurred, and that the three evangelists should have put into the Lord's lips a mistaken prediction, if, "that generation" had passed away when they wrote! This curious blunder, therefore, which has often been cited as an objection, is really an undesigned and startling proof that the writers belonged to the same generation as Jesus.

But now I must remind you that the external evidence never was and never could be the guarantee for the teaching of Jesus. A teaching which comes from God and is intended to save the world, will not depend for its demonstration on documents or on historical witnesses. It must carry its proof in itself. And the overwhelming reason for believing that here we have His teaching is, that the teaching itself, when it is cleared of a few obvious excrescences, due to Judaic or Ebionitic influences or to misunderstandings of the evangelists, stands out in a way which is unmistakable. Never man spake like this Man. That was the impression made from the first. It is the impression made still. If we had only one evangelist, it would be open to us to argue that he had invented

[1] Mark xiii. 30; Matt. xxiv. 34; Luke xxi. 32.

this teaching. In that case he would have been Jesus, and we should have offered to him the homage which we now offer to the Lord. But four writers could not have invented a body of teaching like this, as we shall see directly we look at its characteristics. The Person who produced this teaching is, as such, and whatever He may be styled, the Master Spirit to whom the ages bow down in adoration. The nineteenth as the first century finds that it is impossible to get beyond it.[1]

This conviction grows on every one who makes a complete study of the whole. It will grow upon each of us, I trust, as we proceed. But I may so far anticipate as to state three at any rate of the conclusions which are necessarily reached by such a study.

1. First of all, though the teaching comes to us apparently in broken fragments, it requires but small ingenuity to piece the fragments together, and to trace the outlines of the complete whole which existed in the mind of Jesus.

In the ruined Abbey of St. Albans the restorers found innumerable fragments of carved and painted stone trodden into the ground behind the chancel. When these were collected and patiently pieced together the shrine of the saint was recovered, which

---

[1] Professor G. J. Romanes remarked that the strongest evidence for Christianity was " the absence from the biography of Christ of any doctrines which the subsequent growth of human knowledge—whether in natural science, ethics, political economy, or elsewhere—has had to discount. This negative argument is really almost as strong as is the positive one from what Christ did teach."—*Thoughts on Religion*, p. 157.

stands now in its completeness, a visible proof that the fragments had originally belonged to the whole. In the same way we are able to take the scattered utterances and thoughts of Jesus—many of them individually are found of course in other teachers— and to fit them together, until a lovely and harmonious structure of doctrine rises before our eyes. That some of His thoughts are anticipated by Jewish and Ethnic thinkers does not detract from His originality, because that consists not in isolated truths, but in the remarkable doctrine in which they take their appropriate and articulated place.

Let us vary the illustration. In the discourses which have come down to us we see only one star or one constellation at a time, while the greater part of the sky is obscured with clouds. But as we come to map out the points of light which are from time to time revealed, we discover that the wide span of starry heavens is over us. In His mind everything is complete and consistent, whether He is touching on one part or another at any particular time.

2. But this leads us to notice another peculiarity of His method. He never argues or reasons, as if He were seeking for truth, and arriving at it by the ordinary processes. He simply asserts and declares. *I say unto you*, is the tone of His teaching, all the more remarkable because He is so strangely meek and lowly in heart. Thus it is what Beyschlag calls "the mother speech of religion." It is always as if the reservoirs were up in the heavens, and under His supreme control. He smites the rock as He will, and the waters gush out. We are so familiar

with the manner of the four Gospels that it is difficult to adequately appreciate this feature of the Lord's teaching. But attempt to contrast His way with St. Paul's. Note how He stands at the fountain-head, and, indeed, is the fountain, while St. Paul, with all his divine and eager conviction, with all his inward experience, is still only the chief of those who come to draw water from the fountain; and you begin to realise what a unique mark we have here on the teaching of Jesus. The conviction grows upon you that no one could have invented it.

3. But what are we to say of that chief wonder—viz., the nature of the religion itself which is implied and conveyed by the teaching of Jesus? As we come to grasp this, all misgiving about authenticity fades away. Especially if we have trained ourselves to recognise elements of divine truth in other religions of the world, and can appreciate the finer side of the Buddha, or of Confucius, or of Mahomet, what an overwhelming impression is made on us by the sublimity and simplicity, the truth, obvious at once when stated, but elsewhere not attainable by man, of the religion which Jesus taught! All that is good in other religions has been gathered up and preserved; but all that is local and transitory in them has disappeared. Most important things, unknown to them, are here revealed clear as the sun at noonday. Religion is not a matter of nations or races, but of man. It is not a matter of forms or ceremonies, but of the spirit. It is not a matter of mere outward action, but of the heart. It is not a matter of correct opinion, but of love. "Perfectly moral

and morally perfect," this teaching makes the most humiliating discoveries of human sin and the most exacting demands of holiness. All the notions of holiness entertained by Jew or Buddhist appear formal and tarnished in comparison with what Jesus means, and in His person exhibits, when He speaks of holiness. And yet all is full of compassion and grace. God appears not so eager to convince of sin as to save sinners. The lofty ideal is seen stooping to become real, and to catch up fallen man to itself.

This religion meets the deepest craving of the human heart, because it is the religion of eternal life. It addresses men as the possessors of a lost home which it proposes to restore. It consecrates time and earth by shedding on them the light of heaven and of eternity.

And as for Him who propounds this splendid religious conception, He gives one the impression all the time of gazing into the face of God with untroubled eye and unagitated heart. With no sins of His own to confess, no atonement for Himself to make, He is entirely at leisure to attend to the sinful world. Out of a perfect relation with God flows His teaching like a crystal stream. It flashes with light. It quenches the thirst of the soul. It cuts deep channels, lays bare the heart, breaks it in penitence and tears. No words from human lips were ever like these. Though the whole body of His teaching seems small as the disc of the sun in a summer sky: like the sun, it pervades the world with divine light and warmth, life and love.

In this light, as we abide, we see light. The

Seen becomes a vestibule to the Unseen; the sufferings to which flesh is heir become the discipline in the school of God. We are introduced at once to the kingdom of God, which is *here* like the seed in the soil, and is yet *above* like the harvest of the world, a kingdom which is and is yet to be, homely and comforting to the heart that receives it now, but teeming with sublime expectations for the future.

When we begin to grasp what the truth is which underlies all that He taught, we cannot hesitate about its authenticity. As Rousseau said of the person of Jesus Himself, *l'inventeur en seroit plus étonnant que le héros,* so we may say with confidence that whoever conceived and gave to the world this splendid vision, this interpretation and justification of human life, would be, and must be, the Saviour of the world.

Whence did He derive this teaching? Not from the East, nor from the West. Not from Jerusalem, nor from the ancient Scriptures. If He quotes them it is always as if He were their authority, not they His. *Think not that I came to destroy the law or the prophets; I came not to destroy, but to fulfil.*[1] He fulfilled them only by bringing a kernel out of the husk, and substituting Himself for them. The product of the ancient Scriptures is Judaism. Christianity could not be derived from them.

As no one can suggest any other origin for His teaching, we may, and must, accept His own account of it. *All things have been delivered unto me of my Father; neither doth any know the Father save*

---

[1] Matt. v. 17.

the Son, and He to whomsoever the Son willeth to reveal Him.[1] *My teaching is not mine but His that sent me.*[2]

The teaching is from God; that is the only conclusion we can reach. "See that ye refuse not Him that speaketh from heaven." A charge lies at the door of the Church that she has always been saying, "Hear the Church." How little has she insisted on this prior obligation, "Hear Him!"

But the better day is coming. The new breath is in the air. We have Him as the rock to which we can continually resort. Churches and theologies have failed us and confused us, and mourned their failure and confusion. But Christ remains. He is still in the chair of the Teacher. He still speaks from the Mount.

> Hushed be the noise and the strife of the schools,
>   Volume and pamphlet, sermon and speech,
> The lips of the wise and the prattle of fools;
>   Let the Son of Man teach!
>
> Who has the key of the Future but He?
>   Who can unravel the knots of the skein?
> We have groaned and have travailed and sought to be free:
>   We have travailed in vain.
>
> Bewildered, dejected, and prone to despair,
>   To Him as at first do we turn and beseech:
> "Our ears are all open! Give heed to our prayer!
>   O Son of Man, teach."

---

[1] Matt. xi. 27. [2] John vii. 16.

THE KINGDOM

The kingdom of heaven is at hand (ἤγγικεν—i.e., has come near).—MATT. iii. 2; iv. 17.

THE kingdom of heaven! This was the word on the lips of Jesus when He began to teach. It must have been used by Him every day, and many times a day, during His crowded ministry. And in the last notice we possess of His earthly manifestation, when He was about to ascend to heaven, we find Him for those forty days still "speaking things concerning the kingdom of God."[1]

An idea which thus occupied His mind should surely occupy ours. To understand what He meant by it must be the condition of understanding His teaching as a whole. If we miss the keynote, the master-thought, of a teacher, we are likely to miss everything. And in the case of Jesus the body of doctrine is so compact, so closely related in its several parts, that unless we grasp the ideas which He regarded as central, there is small chance of anything but confusion and misunderstanding.

Yet what part does the teaching about the kingdom of God play in the Church? It is a

[1] Acts i. 3.

strange fact that the beautiful phrase hardly occurs in the New Testament when we have passed out of the Gospel narratives. The Church, broadly speaking, has reached a tacit resolution to ignore the phrase, or else to exploit it. If the words have been used they have borne a meaning far removed from the meaning of Jesus.

The kingdom of God has been understood as a synonym for the Catholic Church. St. Augustine turned the mind of Europe in that direction. Or it has been understood as a periphrasis for the life of the redeemed after death. Protestants have generally accepted this explanation. But nothing can be more evident to a student of the words of Jesus than this: that His language about the kingdom is not suitable to the Catholic Church, and that to confine His reference to the future life is literally to lose His thought altogether.

It is therefore a melancholy fact that if Christian men were asked suddenly to state what this kingdom of heaven is which absorbed their Master's thought—what this phrase means which sounds out again and again in the records of the great biography—a large number would be able to give no answer at all, and a still larger number would give an answer, which, to say the least of it, was never derived from Him or His words.

Here then, at the outset, we discover how "He spake as never man spake." He was constantly addressing the future as well as the present. His words sought their audience a thousand or two thousand years ahead. His ideas had to lie, like a seed-corn in a mummy's hand, waiting millenniums, until they could enter appropriate soil and germinate.

He spoke of the kingdom of heaven. None who heard Him could ever forget the phrase. No one could record His utterances without constantly setting it down. But because many remembered and recorded, it did not follow that they understood. They were far from understanding. They are of small help to us in the matter. When we want to know what Jesus meant, it is useless to ask the Church or the Fathers; it is not enough even to ask the apostles. We must ask Him. The apostles missed some shades of His meaning, the Fathers more, the Church, for weary centuries, lost it altogether. The rosy colours of the dawn faded into the light of common day. The world under a Christian name grew sick and weary again. Theologies waxed and waned. Faith became stale, flat, and unprofitable. To-day a *Christian* country is one in which a majority of the people appear absolutely indifferent to religion; a majority of those who are not indifferent are without enthusiasm, without passion, without zeal; while the most earnest are usually sectarian rather than religious, capable only of interest in their Church, or their system, or their shibboleth. And why? Because we have ignored what He means by the kingdom of heaven. We have allowed ourselves to be deprived of the key of His teaching, and we cannot unlock the door.

But, says some one in protest, all Christians pray again and again in every prayer, public and private, Thy kingdom come! How ridiculous it is to say that we do not know what is meant by the kingdom! But let me be understood. I bring no accusation against the brethren. Of course I know that many who use the phrase attach a meaning to it. But what I venture to assert is, that the meaning is for the most part not the meaning of Jesus. It is the meaning of evangelical hymns, or it is the meaning of Hildebrand, or it is, essentially, the meaning which prevailed in Judaism when Jesus came, the meaning which He laboured to subvert. For we must come now to close quarters, and observe how He borrowed the phrase from the religious language of the day, and *how He transformed it*. Unhappily we have kept it more or less untransformed!

I. He took the phrase from the language of His own day. We know that since the time of the Maccabees the Book of Daniel had been among the most popular books of devotion in Judaism. Jesus was well acquainted with it, and frequently employed expressions from it. Indeed, the opulent symbolism and the gorgeous diction of the book might well give it currency among a religious people, whose religion was of an external and terrestrial type. There one reads: "In the days of those kings shall the God of heaven set up a kingdom which shall never be destroyed, nor shall the sovereignty thereof be left to another people; but it shall break in pieces and consume all these kingdoms, and it shall stand for ever." And "I saw in the night visions, and, behold, there came with the clouds of heaven One like unto a son of man, and He came even to the Ancient of days, and they brought Him near before

Him. And there was given Him dominion and glory and a kingdom, that all the peoples, nations, and languages should serve Him: His dominion is an everlasting dominion, which shall not pass away, and His kingdom that which shall not be destroyed."[1]

This kingdom, which every pious Jew identified with the aggrandisement of his own nation, coloured the patriotism, and excited the expectation, of all who were waiting for Messiah. In all the circles of Jewish orthodoxy it was a topic of discussion, and there was a prayer current, called the Kaddish: "May He shortly cause His kingdom to come!" Thus, John the Baptist, whom all the people counted a prophet, was frequent in his proclamation of the coming kingdom. It was a designation of a good and religious person like Joseph of Arimathæa, "who also himself was looking for the kingdom of God."[2] It was an eager question among the Pharisees "when the kingdom of God should come?"[3] It was a theme of conversation even at a dinner-table, and a devout mind in the Pharisaic coterie would say, as well as feel, "Blessed is he that shall eat bread in the kingdom of God."[4]

It is not so easy for us to penetrate into the mixed and frequently turgid associations of the phrase in the popular mind. There were some, no doubt, who expected a manifested theocracy—a glorious and blessed reign of God over Israel, extending in ever wider circles of conquest to the uttermost ends of

---

[1] Dan. ii. 44, vii. 13, 14.   [2] Mark xv. 43.
[3] Luke xvii. 20.   [4] Luke xiv. 15.

the earth. Their idea was that the nations would become proselytes of the Gate, and the Law of Moses would go out from Jerusalem as the religious code of mankind. It was in itself a fine, if rather grandiose, conception. But as it shaped itself in the common mind, among a fallen and subject race, with proud and bitter memories of the past, it was very far from admirable. Indeed, it was not distinguishable from a narrow and egotistic Chauvinism.

The ordinary Israelite in the crowds whom Jesus addressed probably entertained ideas of this kind: his eye was on the legendary glories of the kingdom in the days of David and Solomon; he exercised his imagination on memories of sacked cities, rebels put under the harrow, provinces annexed. No book of the Bible was more palatable to him than that of Esther, and at the feast of Purim he fed his heart on the story of the persecuted Jews " standing for their lives " in Shushan and throughout the Persian provinces, and slaughtering their enemies by the myriad. Or he pictured to himself the Roman Empire, like that image of iron and clay struck to the dust by the mysterious stone; and that stone was Israel. He was persuaded that the Jew should become the head of the nations and not the tail. Jerusalem and not Rome should be the capital of the earth. Jehovah should take the place of Jupiter Capitolinus. As in his own time all the tribes of Israel gathered and went up to Jerusalem for the stated feasts, so, with the coming of Messiah, should all mankind go up. Israel would be the priesthood of the world, and would occupy the kind of position which historically has been realised by the Pope and the hierarchy of the Western Church.

In a word, what the Jew understood by the kingdom of God was practically what Europe has known for many centuries now as the Roman Church, with this minor difference, that the Pope, cardinals and priests would all be Jews.

These visions of splendour, of conquest, of vengeance and gratified ambition, tinged always with triumphant religious zeal, filled the minds of the people. John the Baptist was not free from them, as his puzzled and disappointed deputation to Jesus shows. And they gave body and passion to the prayer that the kingdom might come.

II. Now Jesus took the familiar phrase, *and transformed it.*

The announcement of the Baptist. He makes His own word for word.[1] But so far from using it in the popular sense, so far even from accepting the Baptist's view of the matter, He made it the main business of His teaching to read into the words a wholly different, and yet an obviously truer, meaning. Using parables for those who were not yet advanced enough to understand—and few of us even now are sufficiently advanced for Him to lay aside parables altogether—but seizing every opportunity of explaining " the mysteries of the kingdom " to those who were able to receive,[2] He spent laborious hours and days in vindicating the grand idea by entirely disentangling it from the worldly expecta-

---

[1] Matt. iii. 2 ; Matt. iv. 17.
[2] Matt. xiii. 11 ; Mark iv. 11.

tions, the national prejudices, and the materialistic interpretations, which were current, and have been current, among men. The boldness of this move is incredible. It is almost as if some strong wise teacher were to arise among us to-day, when the air is thick with schemes of social reconstruction, and were to address Socialists possessed with impossible dreams, pressing crude and external reforms, with the words: "Socialism is at hand; I have come to establish it on earth"; and then were to proceed to explain that Socialism would be realised by every one becoming unselfish, unmercenary, and filled with the spirit of love. Such a teacher would be howled down by Socialist leaders to-day. The Preacher of the kingdom of God, in the right sense of the word, was crucified by those who professed to belong to the kingdom of God in His day. For mark the astounding and radical change He made!

He did not for a moment deny that the Jews were, in the Old Testament sense, the kingdom of God. No one was ever more patriotic than Jesus. He was the first to admit the spiritual supremacy of Judaism among the faiths of the world. The Jew knew what he worshipped, for salvation was of the Jews. Israel were the children at the Father's table, whose bread must not be cast to the dogs. But that was in the Old Testament sense. A new day was dawning. *I say unto you that many shall come from the east and the west, and shall sit down with Abraham, Isaac and Jacob, in the kingdom of heaven, but the sons of the kingdom shall be cast forth* *into the outer darkness.*¹ And to the national representatives He said: *The kingdom of God shall be taken away from you and shall be given to a nation bringing forth the fruits thereof.*²

In a word the kingdom of heaven was not hereditary or national at all. Such kingdoms were from the nature of the case kingdoms of earth not of heaven. The kingdom of heaven was moral and spiritual; and the conditions of entrance were of the same quality.

First, always first, all important, is a state of the soul. How reluctant men are always to be reminded of this! If it is a matter of donning a uniform and fighting, or of adopting a party cry and shouting, we are all very ready at once to enter the kingdom and get the benefit of it. But this suggestion of an inward preparation chills us to the marrow. Yet, *blessed are the poor in spirit for theirs is the kingdom of heaven,* people *who mourn, the meek, they who hunger and thirst after righteousness, the merciful, the pure in heart, the peacemakers, they who suffer for righteousness' sake*—these are the true sons of the kingdom.³

What! on this showing hardly any one, Jew or Christian, can be in the kingdom of heaven. Yet, there is the law of the Sermon on the Mount, written in imperishable letters. Moses could break in pieces the tables of stone, but this table cannot be broken. The kingdom of God is a state of the soul, an inward relation between God and the souls God has made, and a course of earthly conduct which

---

¹ Matt. viii. 12.   ² Matt. xxi. 43.   ³ Matt. v. 3.

results from this relation. And as a state of the soul is not produced by the pomp of officials, the pageantries of courts, the threats of armies, apocalypses, terrors, and other methods which have made much noise in the world, the kingdom of heaven has nothing to do with these. It does not employ them; except indirectly it is not affected by them. Thus even the most gifted prophets of the old *régime* were a little wide in their calculations. They, including the last, John the Baptist, anticipated an apocalyptic demonstration, a tremendous crisis, a sudden coming of Messiah to His temple; they pictured Him with a fan in His hand, burning the chaff with unquenchable fire, gathering the wheat into His garners. He disappointed all these expectations by the turn that He gave to the idea of the kingdom. So astonishing was the contrast between what he expected and what he saw that the Baptist himself was half sceptical. For, here the kingdom was coming, as it were, without any observation. There was no immediate separation between the good and the bad, no harvest of ingathered grain, with piles of the burning chaff. But it was all very quiet and gradual, like leaven working in the dough, or like a seed sown silently in the ground. A mere *word*—not flashing swords and gathering hosts—a mere word was flung broadcast over varying soils, to be baffled, to be rejected, to be destroyed, to make its potent way. How unexciting it looked! No king, then, in this kingdom of heaven! Nothing that we should call a king, until dismissing all ideas of common kingship, crowns, arms, and the glory of conquests, we can understand

> That to guide nations in the way of Truth,
> By saving doctrine and from error lead
> To know, and knowing, worship God aright,
> Is yet more kingly.

Yes, all expectations were frustrated; the kingdom of God was receiving a totally new signification.

III. What was the new signification? According to Jesus, heaven is a state in which the will of God is ideally done, and earth is a state in which the will of God is habitually violated. The kingdom of heaven comes to earth just in proportion as the rebellious wills of men are replaced by the acknowledged will of God. Jesus was Himself the first man who ever on earth did completely the will of God; with Him therefore the kingdom of heaven came to earth. For the first time in human history the finger of God was working absolutely through a human being, and for that reason he could say, *The kingdom of God is upon you.*[1]

The idea is very simple, but everything is involved in it. The sincere and practical recognition that God is sovereign; the complete inward acceptance of His sovereignty; the mode of life which results from this recognition, and this acceptance; that is the kingdom of heaven. It is possible to analyse the idea into two component parts, but the parts are not divided. One may discern, *first*, a relation to

---

[1] Matt. xii. 28; Luke xi. 20.

God, loyalty, obedience, love, such as Jesus manifests in His fellowship with the Father ; *second*, a relation with men, unselfish, affectionate, rich in benignant service, such as Jesus displays in all His earthly life. That is the kingdom of God.

Thus from the moment that Jesus began, not only, like John the Baptist, to preach, but in His own flawless person to manifest, this ideal relation of the human soul with God and man, the kingdom began to come. Immediately eager souls were smitten with the love of it, and sought to possess it as besiegers seek to force their way into a walled city.[1] For to see this kingdom is to desire. Already, from the first day of His manifestation, there are several in it, and the least in it is at once greater than John the Baptist, though he was the greatest born merely of woman. The prophets were not free from turgid, earthly, and unregenerate ideas. But every one as he enters the kingdom lays these aside, and lives only in the Spirit.[2]

But while the coming of the kingdom began at once with Jesus, the kingdom could only come by slow degrees, by more and more. How could it be otherwise than gradual when *whosoever does not receive the kingdom of God as a little child shall in no wise enter therein*.[3] Not many, and they only by throes and travail, become as children. Slowly, but surely, the kingdom will come and the end will be reached. The seed sown in weakness and secresy will be raised in power. Out of the piled sheaves

---

[1] Luke xvi. 16.   [2] Matt. xi. 11.
[3] Mark x. 15 ; Luke xviii. 17.

of human history the children of the kingdom will be gathered, *and they will inherit the kingdom prepared for them from the foundation of the world.*[1]

How lovely is the coming of the kingdom, utterly unlike the coming of earthly sovereigns, and the establishment of thrones on a land made slippery with blood.

A farmer whose fields lay on the undulating slopes of the Cheviots, a man careless, earthbound, sordid, was out early one spring morning, when the ploughs were in the furrow. In a hollow of the hills he found himself alone. All the hedgerows were quick and green. All the birds were singing. Soft white clouds moved across the sky like a procession of dancing children. Suddenly a thought smote him: "Everything I see and hear is praising God—everything except *me*—I am not, I know not how." It was the seed of the kingdom that had fallen into his heart from heaven:

> God taught his heart
> To bear its part
> And join the praise of Spring.

In such a way, silent, potent, unobserved, as the spring works in the bound bosom of the ground, comes the kingdom of God.

[1] Matt. xxv. 34.

THE SON OF MAN

DAN. vii. 13, 14

WHEN one dwells upon the exquisitely simple and convincing idea which is expressed in the purified term, kingdom of heaven, one might be tempted for a moment to suppose that the truth stands out of itself, on its own footing, sufficient, irrespective of Him who announced it. One does not immediately notice that the same truth enunciated by the Baptist, or preached by St. Paul, would not have accomplished the object. There has always been a danger of forgetting that the all-important factor was the *manifestation of the kingdom in a person who completely embodied it.* The world has not wanted prophets and apostles who have asserted that all religion lies in doing the will of God,

> In la sua voluntade è nostra pace.

But what up to the time of Jesus was wanting to the world was the exhibition of the will of God done, and the religious power which flows out of it.

More than once in the Christian centuries men have attempted to preach the kingdom of God which

Jesus preached, leaving out Jesus who preached it. This disastrous omission, however, can never be allowed by one who is determined to study and to understand the teaching of Jesus in its entirety. For in that teaching, next to the constant exposition of the kingdom of heaven nothing occupies a more constant and a more prominent place than the exposition of Himself. Jesus is occupied in offering and explaining His own person to mankind. This is done with such modesty and with such exquisite delicacy—self-assertion is so remote from His character and His method—that a careless reader of the first three, or, as they are called, the Synoptic Gospels, might easily overlook this most remarkable feature of His teaching.

And here let us observe how humorously perverse the human mind is in arguing against its chief good. The divinity of Jesus is assailed in the same breath on two self-contradictory pretexts : *first*, because in the Synoptic Gospels He does not assert His divinity, and *second*, because in the Fourth Gospel He is represented as asserting it. In the latter case it is said, " This man bears record of Himself, His record is not true." In the former case it is said, " He does not bear record of Himself; if He were divine He would have done so." Wonderful to state, the course which He actually pursued was precisely adapted to meet both these objections.

We will at present leave the Fourth Gospel out of account, for it obviously stands in a category apart. But in the Synoptic Gospels He adopts a mode of self-designation, or self-revelation, which, from its very peculiar character, is one of the most striking proofs that could be given of His unique nature. It is this: He chose a title which in its simplest meaning was the Hebrew synonym for man, but in its literary application was identified with the promised deliverer and saviour whom Israel was expecting. Determined to check all the false and materialistic hopes which clustered about the name, Messiah; determined to gain recognition by purely spiritual and moral claims which were the very essence of His work; determined therefore to show Himself only to those who had eyes to see, and at all costs to avoid a premature recognition from those who were spiritually unsuitable, He called Himself by the designation SON OF MAN. Nothing could be simpler than that. Nothing could be more significant. But He held in His own hands the power of declaring its significance.

It is very remarkable that men have been content to read the Gospels for generations without even seriously inquiring why Jesus assumed this singular designation. And when the inquiry was suggested the most strained and far-fetched interpretations were offered. Yet a devout mind, using the Scriptures alone as an aid, might quickly arrive at a conclusion. And how is it likely that we should understand the person and teaching of Jesus before we have taken the trouble to examine the title by which He desired to be known? Could it have been a chance or a meaningless freak, that He spoke of Himself as the Son of Man?

I. *The Origin of the Name.* Every student of

Scripture is aware that the expectations of the kingdom of God in Israel were always connected more or less distinctly with a Person who was eventually to come, and to be *anointed* for the work of establishing the reign of God on the earth. The actual title of The Anointed, in Hebrew The Messiah, in Greek The Christ, does not occur in any specific connection with the Promised One in the canonical Scriptures of the Old Testament. Taken from an obscure passage in the Book of Daniel, however, it became familiar in certain apocryphal writings, like the Book of Enoch, and was in constant use among the pious Jews who waited for the Hope of Israel. In the more ancient writings the idea was developed irrespective of any uniform and exclusive name. More particularly the magnificent prophecy of the Exile which forms the second part of Isaiah worked out the pathetic picture of the Lord's servant, who through suffering and reproach would establish a world-wide reign. And in the last genuine prophecy of the Old Testament occurred the startling promise: "Behold I send my messenger, and he shall prepare the way before me; and the Lord whom ye seek shall suddenly come to His temple, and the messenger of the covenant whom ye delight in, behold he cometh, saith the Lord of Hosts."[1]

After the Captivity, it would seem, the thought of Israel turned back to the monarchy which was now no longer a fact but a memory. Reading and composing Davidic Psalms, inspired men pictured the promised deliverer of the nation as another David.

[1] Malachi iii. 1.

And in the last century B.C. there was a widespread expectation that a scion of the royal house would ascend the throne which had been vacant for five hundred years and reign in Jerusalem as David or Solomon had done.

"We know that Messiah cometh" was the great religious thought of that day. The mysterious forecasts of Isaiah and of the elder prophets were in the background. In the forefront was the vision of a conquering hero, who, if a teacher to lead into all truth, like another Moses, should still more be a captain of armies like David, and a successful vindicator of his country's independence against foreign oppression, like Judas Maccabæus.

It is evident that during the long quiet years in Nazareth, surrounded by these religious aspirations of His people, some of them comparatively pure, but most of them turgid and unspiritual, the conviction deepened in the heart of Jesus that He Himself was the Person whom the prophets had dimly foreseen, whom the nation was eagerly expecting. "The narrative of His baptism," says a brilliant modern writer,[1] "with which the Gospels begin His public life, is nothing but the birth history of this consciousness, His awakening at God's touch to a clear sense of it, the anointing of the secret Child of God to be the Son of God in the Messianic sense."

He knew that He was Messiah, the only Messiah that should ever come to meet the desire of the ancient seers, and to satisfy the ambitions of His

[1] Beyschlag, *New Testament Theology*, i. 58.

contemporaries. But He could not claim or use the name Messiah, because the notions which clung to the name in the minds of the people were for the most part absolutely misleading, and as far as possible removed from the purpose of His mission. He would not—He could not without endangering His work—be known as Messiah, until there were people who had the true Messianic ideas. But this meant, notwithstanding all the prophets had written and pious souls cherished, that He had to create in the minds of men the true idea of what Messiah was to be, before He could make known to the world *I that speak unto you am He.*

Thus He was, on the one hand, obliged to declare to His nation that He was their Messiah, The Christ; and He was, on the other hand, prevented from even mentioning at present the misleading name. It was necessary, therefore, to keep His claim before those whom He chose as the depositories of His self-revelation, in such a form that it would be without any ambiguity for an inquiring and enlightened spirit; and yet He must not say anything to those who were still in a circle of false conceptions. This purpose He accomplished by the title that He assumed. For in the popular and widely read Book of Daniel there was a vision of the worldly kingdoms under the image of a lion, a bear, a leopard, and an unnamed beast, which were to be displaced by "one like a son of man coming in the clouds of heaven," and assuming the dominion of all the earth. Here the Hebrew periphrasis for man was used in a specific and suggestive sense. The outside hearer of His discourses might well carelessly assume that the term was only an expression of humility, as when a speaker to avoid egotism styles himself "the individual that is addressing you." But the inner circle, who had ears to hear, would inevitably inquire, who is this Son of Man? What does He mean by adopting the phrase? And with recollections of Daniel and Enoch they would be gradually led to the right surmise and the anticipated confession.

About fifty times in the Synoptic Gospels does Jesus call Himself the Son of Man. It is perhaps fair to assume that in the early days of His ministry, before Peter's memorable discovery, and in that more exoteric teaching which forms the substance of the first three Gospels, Jesus habitually employed this designation for Himself. It is very simple, and yet how dignified it is! Is it not strange that we have been so indifferent to the inquiry, What was implied in the dignified, simple, self-chosen name of Jesus?

II. *The Meaning of the Name.*—Before we proceed to consider what is implied in this proudly humble name, we must observe that it did not survive in the teaching of the Church. And here is one of the many proofs that the Synoptic Gospels are of a primitive date and come from the immediate group of the first hearers and eye-witnesses. Even when the Fourth Gospel was written, the term, which had long ago served its purpose, was no longer in use, and accordingly the evangelist prefers for the most part the more dignified *Son of God*. This is only an inference from the proportion of usage. In the

Synoptics of course Jesus calls Himself with sufficient distinctness the Son of God.[1] And no one can fail to see that where He employs the term the meaning differs *toto cœlo* from the loose and general way in which angels, magistrates, Israel and individual Israelites, are called sons of God by Old Testament writers.[2] In the Fourth Gospel, on the other hand, He in several important places calls himself the Son of Man.[3] But, broadly speaking, the designation is a proof of very primitive and apostolic records. When believers came to recognise that Jesus was the Son of God, the dazzling fact possessed them almost to the exclusion of humbler ideas. The earliest struggles of the Church, it must be remembered, were not to assert His divinity, which was never questioned, but to maintain His true humanity, which seemed to vanish in the effulgence of divine glory.

If the name, however, was not maintained in the Church it is none the less to be carefully studied as an integral part of His own teaching. And we must now question it to learn what it necessarily implied.

On the one hand, as has already been suggested, His choice of the name may, and probably did, imply that unassuming humility which is an unfail-

---

[1] Matt. xi. 27, and the parables of the vineyard and of the marriage feast of the Son; *cf.* Matt. xii. 6; Matt. xxii. 2.

[2] See Gen. vi. 1; Job i. 6, ii. 1; Ps. lxxxii. 6; Ex. iv. 22; Deut. xiv. 1; Hos. i. 10; *cf.* Ps. ii. 7; 2 Sam. vii. 14; Ps. lxxxix. 27.

[3] John iii. 13, 14; v. 27; vi. 27, 53, 62; viii. 28; xii. 23; xiii. 31.

ing mark of true greatness. We recognise the paltriness of any delight in titles and baubles of that kind. No really significant or important person ever cared to be my-lorded, or to catch the eye of the vulgar with a coronet rather than a character. Jesus certainly had no desire to be called a king.[1] And in choosing the plain title *Son of Man* He probably showed this characteristic of greatness. We may also observe a lovely light thrown on His nature by the fact that He, in using a term which not only indicates humanity, but also, it would seem from its suggestions elsewhere, some of the weakness and limitations of humanity, desired to identify Himself with us as men. He had no inclination to affright us or shame us with His splendour. Rank and title dazzle and draw a crowd. But it is humanity which attaches men. It is the unpretentiousness of the approach, it is the Son of Man reminding us in the first instance that He is a man like ourselves, this it is which wins upon us all.

But with the passage in Daniel before our eyes the reverse side of the title is equally unmistakable. There, as the vision declared, the one like the Son of Man comes in the clouds of heaven. His origin, therefore is not earthly. He comes also to establish a kingdom which, in contrast with the successive empires of the world, is to stand for ever. Nor does he, like even the greatest kings, Rameses, Nebuchadrezzar, Alexander or Cæsar, found a crumbling dynasty of a few generations, himself crumbling into dust before his transient throne has perished. The

[1] John vi. 15.

Son of Man, in the vision, is heir to a regal dignity which he will keep in his own hands through generations.

With these suggestions of the passage from which He selected His name, certainly His stupendous claims were implicit from the first, though the time had not come to make them explicit. He wished to hint that a being not beginning with the earth, nor ending with it, a being of quite another order, was there among men as a Son of Man. He could found the kingdom of heaven, because He alone came from heaven and could return thither. He alone, if we use the other form of the phrase, could establish the kingdom of God, because He alone was akin to God, and had come from God, and was at home with the Ancient of days.

Thus very much was implicit, though little was at first recognised, in the title. But keeping the name —the Son of Man—before His immediate adherents, He began to unfold its meaning to them in a way that at present He could not do to the careless outside hearers; this He did by unveiling Himself in all the simple grandeur of His moral perfection, and all the astounding power of His spiritual life. It was of course a gradual process, but little by little the conviction was wrought in the mind of one at least of His intimates, the conviction which found expression in that memorable utterance, the pivot and turning-point of the Synoptic narrative, when Jesus asked, *Who do men say that I the Son of Man am?* and Peter answered, flinging away the false notions of his race and of his generation, and obtaining at

just one flashing glimpse of the truth which Jesus
had been all along unfolding, "Thou art the Messiah,
the Son of the living God,"[1] as if he meant to say in
a word, "I see it now, Son of Man means Messiah,
and that in Thee means Son of God."

That was the starting-point of all. That was the
true foundation. That was the guarantee of the
kingdom of heaven. Certainly it was coming to
earth. For not only had He who embodied it come,
but now one ordinary human being had recognised
who He was and had avowed a conviction that this
pure, holy, humble, simple being, engaged perpetually
with His Father's will, He and not a sceptred
monarch or a blood-stained conqueror, was the Hope
of Israel, the Founder of the kingdom.

Here let us pause for a moment, and allow a
secondary suggestion of this unique title to distil
upon our spirits like the dew. The word Humanity,
with all its sorrowful hints of weakness and vice, is
dear to our ears. *Homo sum, humani nihil a me
alienum puto* is one of the few sayings in Latin literature which have a flavour of divine inspiration. As
the world grows old man draws to his fellow-man ;
by a subtle understanding men recognise that they are
related ; and, standing together, they view the perish-
able earth as a thing apart from them. "Man" has
been uttered and chanted by the accumulating centuries ; and more and more the word carries in it the
thought of "God." Some day it will be impossible to
mention the word Man without waking the echo, God.

[1] Matt. xvi. 16 ; Mark viii. 30 ; Luke ix. 20.

The sorrow of history is the comparative rareness of humanity in it. It is as if humanity were only born by degrees. Those repulsive brute empires, Babylon, Media, Persia, Macedon, though they relate to men, are they not intrinsically inhuman? Were they not secular illustrations of "man's inhumanity to man"? Nay, even now, with the world before our eyes, can we pretend that any governments outside the borders of Christianity are really human? Is the Turk human? Is the Chinese Mandarin human? Was Lobengula human? These are men, but they are not human. The ape and the tiger are stronger in them than the man. Our own government is partially human, because it is partially Christian. Some faint aroma of mercy and justice and truth is in our throne-rooms and State departments because the Son of Man has passed through them.

But the blessed actual reign of the Son of Man, His appropriate sphere, where willing subjects love Him and express His will, stands in contrast with all earthly governments, because it is absolutely humane. It has no touch of savagery in it. It has no Holy Office of the Inquisition, no High Commissions and Star Chambers, no insolence of tyrannical priests, no savage engines of social ostracism and contempt, no delight in crushing sensitive souls by terrors and bribes, by frowns and fawning smiles. In His kingdom it would be impossible for a landlord to hound out a tenant because he did not go to church, or for a priest to affright a Dissenter with threats of hell. All this is as remote from Him as humanity is from inhumanity. Thus the reign of the Son of

Man seems feeble by comparison with worldly forces, and men seriously believe that He would be worsted if He lost the revenues of the Church, or if these engines of tyranny were not employed to make men think alike. But the Roman Empire perished, and the reign of Jesus survived. This gentle impalpable power of meekness, sympathy, love, is stronger than armies of State. The reign of the Son of Man will be the only government which ultimately survives.

For, to touch one more suggestion, the sovereign is the Son of Man *coming out of heaven;* that is to say that ideal man is in heaven, cherished there in prophetic assurance. The blessed region of the Unveiled Face, that shining hierarchy of

> Thrones, dominations, virtues, princedoms, powers,

where the bright ranks of unfallen spirits lead up to the central Being of Light and Love unapproachable, is not complete without man. In the heart of God, man has a place of which he cannot be disseized. Out of heaven issues the Son of Man to fetch men thither. To that upper air we in a sense belong.

His very name delivers a message to us: " Dark, defiled, demon-haunted spirit, black with venom and despair, you, the worst of men, you are a man therefore the Son of Man does not despair of you. Rather, He has set His heart on saving you. He has come to seek and to save that which is lost."

This is no wrathful prophet, no mouth of denunciation and anathema. It is the Son of Man. All hope, all comfort, all divine redemption nestles in the word.

THE FATHER

MATT. xi. 27

THE difference between Jesus and us—one might say, if we see what it implies, the whole difference—is that He is sinless, and we are sinful. *Humanum est errare.* Sin enters so essentially into the very definition of man, that but for the one historical exception we should be inclined to say that wherever man is, sin is. In the abstract it does not seem beyond the range of fancy to conceive a sinless human being. But to give it concrete expression appears to be impossible. One cannot find details to embody the idea. There is in the pigments and the brush some element which vitiates the portrait. While, therefore, we may maintain as a theory that a man might be sinless, experience is too strong for us, and we are convinced that no one actually is.

But, as Ullmann showed, in that treatise of his which remains of permanent value, the sinlessness of Jesus is established in the region of history at once by the faithful photographic portrait presented in the Gospels, and by the self-consciousness of Jesus expressed or implied by all His recorded words. Here then can be no question of invention, or legendary growth, or mythical construction, because the idea itself is not conceivable except as the reflection of a concrete fact. It is not an idea that one brings to the Gospels: rather it is an idea which comes for the first time out of the Gospels. It does not lie on the surface. But slowly the impression gains upon the student as he seriously and reflectively handles the material: This is a man without sin. It is misleading to quote texts. Nothing but a detailed examination, such as Ullmann has given, conveys the proof in its impressive completeness. It is but the epitome of all He did and said, when He exclaims *This is my blood shed for the remission of sins*, implying that sin of His own was not in His thought, but that He was free to undertake the redemption of the world from sin, unembarrassed by those hindrances which other men would find in their own sinfulness.

Now when we meet with this one life, which, contrary to all human experience, is free from sin, we are tempted to say, Surely He is not human. We take refuge in an indefinite term; we say He is superhuman. That, historically speaking, was the first thought of the Church. In Docetism and Apollinarianism the conviction found different expressions, that His human life was more or less illusory. The *Logos* took the place of the human soul; the flesh and blood were not realities, but phantasmal. Conscious of sin ingrained in us, we look with incredulity on a nature like our own which is yet unconscious of sin.

But the Church had firm ground to tread on when she met these heretical tendencies by the assertion of Christ's full humanity. The Gospel narratives put this point beyond question. Indeed, the strongest argument against the view that the Gospels are a product of the second century lies in the fact that no writer of that period would have ventured to represent Jesus in so thoroughly human a way as the Evangelists represent Him in the Gospels. In these documents He is seen tempted like as we are, subject to all the infirmities of the flesh; not laying claim to omniscience, since He frankly says that He knows not the day or the hour of His return; nor yet to omnipotence, since He affirms that to sit on His right hand and His left is not His to give. Nay, startling as it sounds to a dogmatic orthodoxy, He declines even the title *Good*, which is incidentally addressed to Him, not, of course, that any could convince Him of sin, still less that He was conscious of it Himself, but because He was so thoroughly aware of His humanity, and of the divine nature which stood over against it, that He could not allow for Himself an appellation which is only appropriate to God. It would have been impossible for Him in any way to express more emphatically His true humanity.

And, indeed, as is coming to be more and more recognised, the dazzling effect produced upon us by the story of His life is not due to superhuman or miraculous elements but to the fact that as a man He lived; that, according to the words of an apostolic writer, "God made Him perfect through suffering"; and that His life was an orderly development from original innocence to completed holiness.

"He was man," say the Gospels. But when the careless unobservant world wishes to add, "like us," it is brought to a sharp stand. No, not like us, because He was without sin. The first thing that strikes us in ourselves is that we are sinful. The fact that grows upon us in Him is that He is sinless.

I. Now the salient passage from which the text is taken implies a truth, which is so simple, so magnificent, so joyful, that mankind seems unwilling to accept it. *Perfect sinlessness in a human being is equivalent to oneness with God.* A human soul without sin finds itself fully revealed as a son to a father fully revealed. In this startling passage we see Father and Son lying open to one another as if an original relation had never been disturbed. They are together in perfect harmony and mutual knowledge. Here is a human soul, a soul unmistakably human, which is "a perfect home of God, a sanctuary undefiled."

Needless to say, we are looking at this subject just now not from the dogmatic, but from the historical, point of view. And we find a human being that differs from all other men in the fact that He is sinless; and in this sinless soul we find a relationship with God, which seeks its nearest earthly analogy in the relationship of father and child. Like an undimmed and unwarped mirror it reflects perfectly the face of God as the Father.

It suggests at once, before we examine any specific words of Jesus on the subject, that God is intrinsically, by His very nature, the Father. If we had never sinned, if we were undimmed and unwarped, that face would be reflected in our hearts; we should have been in that delightful relationship, laid on His bosom, clasped to His heart. We should not have been blindly seeking after God, if haply we might find Him. He would have been there all the time, like our nursing-mother on whom we first opened our eyes. We should not have been figuring idols and demons as the Supreme, trembling before them and propitiating them; we should not have been munching the swine's husks of atheism and agnosticism. If only we had been free from sin and lived free from sin, we should have known our Father, and been known of Him all along. The king is as it were *revealed to babes;* for of such is the kingdom of heaven. In spite of the integuments of evil which grow up around us as we grow there is in the heart of childhood a sweet vanishing vestige of an original sinlessness, which is to say the least of it as remarkable in experience as the sorrowful counter-fact, original sin. There was a vision about our cradle, a paradise in our nursery, like the picture of man before the serpent tempted Eve. The dark courses of the world had not flowed through us; the poisoned well within us was not yet unsealed. Wordsworth has described that blissful experience of childhood. We have all had glimpses of it, though in later life they are forgotten. No one can read the great Ode on the Intimations of

Immortality without at least a fleeting impression that it records things that each of us has in a manner known.

With Jesus that heavenly state of childhood always continued. What is revealed to babes, and babes alone among men, was revealed unimpeded to Him all through His life. For the floods of the world obtained no entrance, and the well within was not poisoned. Thus when childhood passed into youth, His one thought was, *I must be about my Father's business*,[1] and when the man was prepared for His life task, the confirmatory voice from Heaven was " This is my beloved son in whom I am well pleased." It was all unbroken and continuous to Him, an experience which presents itself in the Gospels so unostentatiously precisely because it was to Him a matter of course, a native and intrinsic fact which acquired emphasis not by contrast with any inward experience of a contrary kind, but only by the contrast which growing acquaintance with the world revealed between His own consciousness and that of other men.

Thus it became plain to Him that He and He alone could reveal the Father to men. Though He never drew a formal contrast between Himself and others, the conviction could not be evaded. He alone was without sin. The intimate fellowship with the Father which filled His soul was without parallel in the hearts of others. And out of this sweet and modest knowledge flowed that exquisite invitation : *Come unto me all ye that labour and are*

[1] Luke ii. 49.

heavy laden, and I will give you rest.[1] As if it were breaking on Him with the joy of a discovery, and He allowed His meek and lowly spirit to leap up at the bliss of it : " Forlorn, blind, scattered children of your Father, prodigal there by the swine trough, proud elder brother, fretting and fuming without, come unto *me;* I can bring you to the bosom of the Father."

II. But when He says *Father*, we must observe that there is an originality and uniqueness in His use of the term, which we may easily miss, from our habit of using a word with many fine gradations of differing signification, until the two ends of the scale are far removed as the poles from one another. It has been said by Prof. Max Müller that there is no religion, which is sufficiently recorded to be understood, that does not in some sense or other apply the term Father to its Deity. In the vague bearings of that fact we may lose what is distinctive in the thought of Jesus. Zeus was the father of gods and men in the Homeric poems. Jehovah in the Old Testament was the father, if not of the individual Israelite, yet of Israel as a whole. " Thou shalt say unto Pharaoh "—ran the message to Moses—" Thus saith the Lord, Israel is my son, my firstborn."[2] And so in Hosea, " When Israel was a child I loved him, and called my son out of Egypt,"[3] and even " In the place where it was said unto them, Ye are not my people, it shall be said unto them, Ye are the sons of the living God."[4]

[1] Matt. xi. 28, following on the text v. 27.
[2] Ex. iv. 22.   [3] Hos. xi. 1.   [4] Hos. i. 10.

"Is Ephraim my dear son? Is he a pleasant child?" we read in Jeremiah, "I do earnestly remember him still."[1] And in the Book of Isaiah, "Thou, O Lord, art our father; our redeemer from everlasting is Thy name;"[2] which is echoed in Malachi, "Have we not all one Father, hath not one God created us?"[3]

In Ecclesiasticus and Wisdom there was, on this as on so many other points, a transition from Old to New Testament ideas. Thus there is a prayer beginning "O Lord, Father and Governor of all my whole life .... Father and God of my life."[4] And the reproach urged against the good man by the wicked is: "He calleth himself the child of the Lord ... he maketh his boast that God is his Father—if the just man be the son of God He will help him."[5] And another prayer runs: "Thy providence, O Father, governeth the ship, for Thou hast made a way in the sea."[6]

But penetrate behind the word to the idea, and it soon appears that there is only a verbal connection between the application of the term Father to God in the Ethnic and Jewish religions, and the use which Jesus makes of it. Broadly speaking, the word was equivalent, in that earlier usage, to Creator; it referred simply to the relation which God might reasonably have with the creatures of His hands. Seldom did it involve such an ethical idea, as when the Psalmist says, "like as a father pitieth his

---

[1] Jerem. xxxi. 20.
[2] Isaiah lxiii. 16.
[3] Mal. ii. 10.
[4] Ecclus. xxiii. 1, 4.
[5] Wisdom ii. 16, 18.
[6] Wisdom xiv. 3.

children so the Lord pitieth them that fear Him." But a spiritual affinity which should unite God and man by a tie of love, and reveal God to man in an actual, immanent, and personal sense, was not dreamed of. When we come to examine carefully what is implied by the words of Jesus, we are left in no doubt. Nothing in any religion approaches this relation of Jesus to the Father. It is absolutely alone. It cannot even be described by terms borrowed from any other quarter; for each expression of it has a complete originality which could not have been anticipated. Everything is perfectly simple and limpid, and, being now very familiar to us, is apt to pass unnoticed. But consider what is implied by the authoritative assertion, *Not every one that saith unto me, Lord, Lord, shall enter into the kingdom of heaven, but he that doeth the will of my Father which is in heaven,*[1] or the majestic, *Every one who shall confess me before men, him will I also confess before my Father which is in heaven,*[2] or the mediatorial intimacy of *Whosoever shall do the will of my Father which is in heaven, he is my brother, and sister and mother.*[3] The confidence of a complete harmony with the Father's thought is expressed in *Every plant which my heavenly Father planted not shall be rooted out,*[4] and of unbroken fellowship with Him in, *My Father which is in heaven revealed it unto thee.*[5] We might continue quoting these references to the Father throughout the Gospels. They are all alike; they are all unlike anything else. A deep inner con-

---

[1] Matt. vii. 21.   [2] Matt. x. 32.   [3] Matt. xii. 50.
[4] Matt. xv. 13.   [5] Matt. xvi. 17.

sciousness unites Him with His Father, in a reverence, a love, a lowly sense of equality which could not be presented in words more distinctly than it is here conveyed by the habitual language of Jesus.

The note which is struck in these sayings of Jesus had never been struck before, nor has it ever been struck since. Even the best, the most saintly, of Christians has hesitated to use the words of assured intimacy which came naturally to His lips. Many of the holiest of the earth habitually speak of the Almighty with a sense of awful distance. They who have caught the spirit and words of Jesus will think and speak of God as our heavenly Father. In the secret passages of the soul a devout man may say specifically " My Father "; but how different is the implication of the "my"! With him it will be a profound submission of spirit, an adoration, a trembling tenderness, which thrills with joy and yet hesitates as it rejoices, to use this bold familiarity with God. In Jesus there is no trace of such a misgiving. What shocked and outraged the Pharisees in His mode of speech was an unmistakable fact, however little it furnished a proper ground of offence. He spoke of the Father, " making Himself equal with God." It was the tone which in England we sometimes hear when a father has lived in close and sympathetic companionship with his son, and the two are comrades and friends. The son behaves to his father with a perfect sense of equality, though with a reverence which is begotten of knowledge.

If therefore we allow ourselves to perceive what is implied by this trait in the self-consciousness of

Jesus, we become aware that the words "My Father" on His lips are in effect a complete theology, a theology which rendered all the elder systems immediately antiquated, a theology which left nothing for later theologies to add. A new idea had glided into the world, and a new possibility was thrown open to man. Whoever saw Jesus, that calm untroubled mirror in which the face of Another was reflected, might henceforth say, as had never been possible before, that he had "seen the Father."

III.—No man could know the Father *save he to whomsoever the Son willeth to reveal Him*. A strange thing happens if a man takes up his position for awhile side by side with Jesus. He sees at once that God is Father, *his* Father, and yet that he is not God's son. A cry will presently escape his lips: "What though God is essentially Father, even my Father, if the width of the heavens is between us, and I see on His face nothing but outraged love and offended majesty?" Nor is it left to the working of his own conscience. Jesus is explicit in assuring him—and us all—that something has to be done, some moral change has to take place, a kind of spiritual birth must be effected *in order that ye may become children of your Father in heaven*.[1]

This double revelation of the mind of Jesus is very remarkable. Doubtless God is our Father. Fatherliness is a quality in Him which we are at liberty to interpret through the best fatherhood we know. *If ye, being evil*, says Jesus, *know how to give good gifts to your children, how much more*

[1] Matt. v. 45, ὅπως γένησθε υἱοὶ τοῦ Πατρὸς ὑμῶν.

shall your Father which is in heaven give good things to them that ask Him.[1] Yes, but sonship is a lost quality in us. The fountains of our filial love are dark with vice, or frozen with pride. They do not flow, or flowing they emit poison. Somehow no man knows the Father save he to whom Jesus reveals Him.[2]

Thus Jesus, directly He opens His lips, begins to make a powerful impression upon us. Man as He is, He belongs to heaven, that better upper region, peopled with happy spirits, where the will of God is done. We belong to earth, where the Will is violated. Or rather we are creatures with two natures in us which strive for mastery, the one earthly, the other heavenly. It is useless to suppose that we can be at home on earth, for we are afflicted with a great *Heimweh*. Yet it is equally idle to think that we can win to heaven. We have but to listen to Him to be assured of this. On the other hand, we have but to listen to Him to be assured of a beneficent purpose within Him. Sinless, He is here to make us sinless; the Son, He is here to make us sons. His words exactly interpret us to ourselves. *What doth it profit a man to gain the whole world and to forfeit his life?*[3] Evidently nothing. Yet, *it is not*

---

[1] Matt. vii. 11.
[2] The filial feeling which seems sometimes to be innate in sweet clear spirits like Rahel, Richter, Emerson, who yet do not share the Christian faith in Jesus, can be explained in the light of the saying (Matt. xi. 27) only by admitting that Jesus "wills to reveal the Father" to some "Israelites in whom is no guile," though they do not as yet recognise the Son."
[3] Mark viii. 36; Matt. xvi. 26.

the will of your heavenly Father, that one of these little ones should perish.[1] And, as He proceeds to unfold us to ourselves and to unfold God to us, so plainly does He present Himself as the reconciliation, the means by which the alienated children can be restored to their Father, that we become intensely alive to the conflict which is raging.

Who can listen to Him long without perceiving that heaven and earth are claiming us! One or the other must win. Behind the death of the body —which is a detail—there awaits the soul of man a glorious ascent or a sad descent. This life would seem to be the parting of the ways, the *punctum discriminis.* How intense becomes the agitation of the question whether one is to arise and return to his Father, or to waste his substance after an irretrievable manner in the ways of debauchery and swine!

[1] Matt. xviii. 14.

SIN

Mark iii. 29, ἔνοχος αἰωνίου ἁμαρτήματος

THE teaching of Jesus on the subject of Sin and its forgiveness is remarkable for this: it avoids all speculation and adheres solely to the practical issue. It would seem, that in comparison with human theologians and preachers, He is more eager to be rid of sin, and less disposed to discuss it. Sinless Himself, and therefore acutely sensitive to its evil and misery, He combats it like a thoroughly healthy doctor, who spends little time in theorising, but is always engaged in a close hand-to-hand conflict with disease.

Theologians are of course persons, like the rest of men, more or less blinded and paralysed themselves by sin. Hence they take a curious interest, an interest which if they were without sin they could not take, in speculating about the origin, the progress, the expiations of sin. They stand by while men are perishing and nicely balance arguments, or rear airy structures in the region of the unknown. Hence they often give the same impression as a demonstrator who is dealing with a sick man, not to cure the patient, but to instruct the student.

This mode of touching sin is entirely alien to the method of Jesus. He has no doctrine about sin in general, nor even about its origin. Whether He shared the current view that it all sprang from the sin of Adam, we are entirely unable to say. He never referred to Adam, nor is it easy to imagine Him handling the theory of original sin which is contained in the Thirty-nine Articles or the Westminster Confession.

Sin was there before Him as an actual fact; and He was there to face and overcome it single-handed.

Yes, single-handed; for He knows nothing of any other beside Himself free from sin. He assumes that every one needs to repent. He even used the keen weapon of irony, in speaking of those *righteous persons which need no repentance*.[1] The very best, most blameless, and most docile of human beings with whom He came into contact, though they might be in a relative sense without guile, needed to be converted and to become as little children before they could enter the kingdom of heaven.[2] They were in the position of an unfortunate servant who owes his master the impracticable sum of £2,400,000.[3] For even if they should succeed in doing all that they ought to do, such is their intrinsic weakness and insufficiency that they would be obliged to approach their Lord with the confession that they were unprofitable servants. Just as surely as He was sinless, all men are sinful.

Now, without forming any theory about sin, Jesus treats it as *a blindness of the soul*. If only the eye

[1] Luke xv. 7.   [2] Matt. xviii. 3.   [3] Matt. xviii. 23, 35.

were in a healthy state—that is, if the organ of spiritual vision were normal, the light of God would stream into the soul as it did with Him.[1] But here lies the mischief. The centre of life—the heart—is wrong. In vain the light from without solicits entrance; it plays on blind eyeballs. The light within is darkness. The goodness which passes muster among the Pharisees, or the religious philosophy of the Scribes, is no better than the blundering of those who know not the law. When the blind leads the blind, leader and led fall into the ditch.

It is only the sinless who sees sin in this way. Men, blundering in their blindness, define it as deeds of omission or commission. Men prescribe religious acts to counterbalance the evil acts. But a sinless soul who sees is aware that the mischief is far deeper than acts; it recognises, therefore, no virtue in acts which only appear religious. The Pharisee offering up florid prayers, with appropriate costume and genuflexion, in the Temple, does not seem so good as the miserable and distressed man, acknowleged by every one to be laden with sin; because this one has at least been making the discovery that he is blind, and in the horror of darkness cries for light.

Now, nothing is more reassuring in the treatment of sin than to find that the physician has not lost all power of discrimination. If Jesus had taught the total depravity of human nature, we should have lost confidence in Him, just as the world has lost confi-

[1] Matt. vi. 22, 23 (Luke xi. 34, 36).

dence in the theology which taught it. It simplifies matters to assume that black and white are the only colours, or to hold that light passes into darkness without any gradual transitions of twilight. For systematic theology assumptions of this kind may be necessary. Indeed, if we are going to give a complete scheme of things, we are bound to simplify the premisses. The complexities of fact would shatter our scheme.

Take the total depravity of human nature for granted, and you have a fine inky background on which to pencil out your wavering lines of light. But this is to make a picture, not to delineate truth. If Jesus had adopted this method, He might have deeply impressed contemporaries, and produced a fuliginous revival. But He would have ceased to be the Master Teacher of the world, the Truth, the luminous, sinless Eye that sees things just as they are. He, as we have seen, recognises that no man is free from sin, but He does not hold that every man is entirely devoid of goodness. He distinguishes. *The good man out of his good treasure bringeth forth good things, and the evil, evil.*[1] He is full of frank delight in a good deed, though it is performed by so heterodox and ill-favoured a person as a Samaritan. Where theology would have been eager to dissect the action and to prove that good works from such a quarter could not really be good, He finds occasion for admiring commendation. *Go thou and do likewise,* is His comment on a deed of mercy which is totally disconnected from all correctness of doctrine. He

[1] Matt. xii. 35.

has a doctrine which is all His own about children—
a doctrine which He could not have held if He had
accepted the popular view of the Fall, or if He had
attached the meaning which has since been attached
to original sin. Speaking of children, He said, *Of
such is the kingdom of God.*[1] It has been thought
possible to explain this saying away, and to show
that He only meant to teach that certain qualities of
childhood—simplicity, trustfulness, buoyancy of heart
—are qualities to be retained in the kingdom of God.
But, praiseworthy as these efforts are to claim Jesus
as a teacher of a doctrine which has made some
stir in the world, our present inquiry is directed
rather to finding out what He taught, as a criterion by
which to judge what has been advanced in His name,
than to hastily insist that all which the Church has
taught shall be in some way or other read into His
words. At present, His simple idea that children
should be allowed to come to Him, because to them
and their like the kingdom of God that He came to
preach belongs, places a wide gap between Him and
those who delight in describing all human beings, as
such, in the language which a prophet employs for a
people in a state of terrible degradation, and on the
eve of their punishment, "The whole head is sick,
and the whole heart faint. From the sole of the
foot even unto the head there is no soundness in it; but
wounds and bruises and festering sores."[2] Indeed,
we have constantly to choose between Christ and
Theology. What has He to do with a grim, coarse
dogma, that sweeps all mankind into one net, makes

[1] Mark x. 14.   [2] Isa. i. 5, 6.

no distinctions between degrees of sin, but consigns multitudes, of every shade of moral turpitude, to the dead level of a fiery lake and the measureless reaches of eternal torture? He recognises the minutest differences, so that stripes few or many will fall in exact proportion to desert.[1] And so sensitive is He to the shades in that which Theology has covered with one broad sweep of black, that He singles out certain cities that had been notorious for their iniquity—Sodom and Gomorrha, Tyre and Sidon—and discovers some elements of good in them, at least in comparison with those unrepentant cities where His own mighty works were done.[2]

We may say, then, that in His estimate of sin there is a discrimination, a balance, a sanity, a delicacy, which cannot be found elsewhere. Men will deny sin altogether, or palliate it, until all moral indignation dies away. Or else they will damn it with loud and thunderous denunciation, making no distinction between a needle-point and a mountain, so that it be sin at all. Consequently, the human treatment of sin is, like sin itself, grotesque and distorted. An extravagance, chilling into indifference or blazing into fanaticism, renders the handling of the subject futile. The human teacher seldom escapes factitious elements. He diminishes or exaggerates. He either makes little of the symptoms or overdoes his indignation. There is the unreality of a stage-play in his methods. But Jesus touches the matter with a sensitive hand, which lightly but firmly follows the contour, with this result: that with His treat-

[1] Luke xii. 47, 48. [2] Matt. xi. 22.

ment, sin stands out just as it is; we are not paralysed with horror, nor lulled with explanatory apologies; it appears hateful enough to set us on overcoming it, yet compassable enough to forbid despair of victory.

It is His tranquil and unexcited analysis of sin which leads us back to the root of evil in the evil thought. We see the rise and progress of sin in the soul, from thought to deed, from deed to habit, from habit to some unpardonable blasphemy or other.[1] In the motions of the heart, as in the springs among the hills, the river of evil has its source. There the arrest must be made. We are not to wait until autumn to see the character of the fruit. The tree is good or bad long before the fruit appears, and with the tree we are concerned.[2] In our text, sin indulged becomes a binding tyranny, from which there is no escape. And in marking the fateful commencements of evil we are always to remember that one may come to an extreme and irreversible pass. Sins of every kind may be forgiven—even a blasphemy against the Son of Man—in this world, or, it is suggested, in the next. But there is a blasphemy against the Holy Spirit which admits of no pardon here or there.[3] He would not particularise or explain. Nothing is gained by a morbid analysis of strange sins. But He would remind those who tread the perilous way that at a certain point, unawares, the foot may touch the descent of an abyss from which there is no return, may reach the valley of Hinnom, where the spiritual

---

[1] Matt. v. 22.   [2] Matt. xii. 33.   [3] Matt. xii. 31, 32.

refuse of the universe burns down in the corruption of worms and the consuming of unquenchable fires.

An excitable Dominican monk, descanting on the torments of hell, will scare the multitude into penances, but will revolt thoughtful men with a sense of extravagance. But the perfectly calm, clear-sighted statement of Jesus on this subject produces a different effect. If He is permitted to speak, and He alone, not only are the acknowledged sinners in Zion afraid, but the most cultivated and the most thoughtful minds detect the note of truth, and are led by the quiet hand into the unquestioned secrets of the spiritual life. Sin is detected, the roots of the plant are dug up. The dread possibility is avoided.

But it is time to notice an element in the teaching of Jesus about sin, which has given rise to some protest, and even to contemptuous rejection. Among the current doctrines of His time was one which identified the origin of Evil with a personal spiritual being, the enemy of human souls, that ceaselessly plots against the happiness and salvation of man. Popular theology recognised this being in the serpent of Eden, and in the one among the sons of God that attempted the destruction of Job. Now while Jesus never for a moment countenanced the vagaries and the legends of the popular theology, it is incontestable that He gave His sanction to the idea as a whole. Evil was in His judgment the work of an Enemy, who sows tares among the wheat. In certain diseases and forms of insanity

He traced the work of this malignant enemy. If He employed the language of the day, and spoke habitually in the pictorial method of parables, still it is impossible to miss this underlying conviction in all His thought, that in the world of nature, and in the course of history, an actual personal power, that is not to be traced up to God, a power that apes God, and is opposed to God, must be recognised as the virtual prince of the present order. Jesus expressly states more than once that He is engaged in a victorious conflict with this power, and is here in the world to destroy his works.[1]

The triviality and childishness of those who have mingled mediæval stories with the teaching of the Bible have given us a natural distaste to the whole subject. But it is part of the discipline of Jesus to teach us to discover the kernel of truth in things which credulity has rendered incredible and folly has made ridiculous.

Yet recognising the *Prince of this world* as He does, Jesus gives no countenance at all to a dualistic theory. Only by entirely ignoring all His words could the Manichean doctrine of an equal strife beween Good and Evil be asserted. To Him, at least, the Sinless One, and to all who in Him enter the kingdom of heaven, the Enemy is a vanquished and enfeebled power, which, like the Devil of popular tales, is almost childish in impotence. There is no question of an equal war between God and the Prince of this world. It is God's world. The prolonged opposition of the Enemy, overcome

[1] The actual expression is from 1 John iii. 8.

by the grace of God, results in a greater good. Instead of regarding Matter or the corporeal elements of man as intrinsically evil, and the realm of the Evil Power, He quite expressly asserts that this Power's realm is the Spirit. Matter is innocent enough. Meats and drinks are to be enjoyed; they cannot defile a man.[1] Asceticism never enters into His thoughts of life, unless it be the asceticism of sorrow, which refuses meat because the heart languishes bereaved. If in the region of the perverted human will the Enemy claims a usurped mastery of the kingdoms of the world and their tawdry glory, he has no control over nature, no rights against God. God sends the sun and the rain. The birds of the air are the subjects of the Father's care. *To God all things are possible.*[2] If the human soul has surrendered its allegiance and chosen the Enemy, still God, who marks the fall of the bird, counts the hairs of the head of his creature man,[3] holds the control of each life within His own hands, and directs even the apparently uncontrolled courses of human history.[4]

If Jesus convinces us of the reality and power of our tempter, it is He who breaks the power, and secures for us the reality of victory.

Thus above all things He teaches the sovereign strength of prayer.[5] The free action of God is never limited, but is determined all along by spiritual and moral considerations of which the prayer of man is

---

[1] Matt. xi. 19; xv. ii.   [2] Matt. v. 45, vi. 26.
[3] Matt. x. 29, 30.   [4] Matt. xxiv. 22.
[5] Matt. vii. 7-11, Mark xi. 24.

always one. What a godless and shortsighted knowledge would describe as "miracles" are therefore no miracles to Jesus. His assumption always is that matter is in God's power, like a tool in the hands of a workman. Undoubtedly God is always guiding the world towards an ideal goal of perfection. The World, and Life, and Time, which filled Shelley with so passionate a melancholy, are to Jesus merely an episode, a pang of birth, an entrance into the order which endures. Behind the dark and local night of human experience shines the illimitable dawn. There awaits the world a *Palingenesia*, a new Genesis, of which the first was but a type. We are baffled who walk always in the black shadow of the night, but He, entering the shadow, never lost the clue of the Eternal Light.

This accounts for the fact that Jesus stood in the presence of sin, free from all the hysterical horror which disqualifies one from undertaking the cure. The Prince of this world reigns for a time, but Jesus reigns for ever. Out of the shadow He summons each beguiled and fallen soul with the grandest offer of mercy, and a free forgiveness for every one who repents. Impossible as it is for unaided sinful men to see it for themselves, Jesus sees, and describes to them, the picture of the Father, an almighty, living, loving reality, who watches and waits for the return of His prodigals, eager to welcome them home. With the one exception above referred to, *all manner of sins and blasphemies wherewith soever they shall blaspheme can be forgiven to men.* It does not seem possible to Jesus to exaggerate the compassion of

God. As long, as wide, as deep as His unchangeable righteousness is His abounding mercy. Thus, where Theology has treated of an angry God, Jesus had dwelt upon a Father longing for His son to come back. Where Theology has treated sin as guilt, Jesus seems rather to regard it as a grim disease. Consequently we miss in Him that irritation and censoriousness which mark men's treatment of sin, as we miss in men that extraordinary freedom and unconditional alacrity of pardon which we find in Him.

Our attempts to preserve the doctrine of Atonement, and not to slight the meaning of Christ's sacrifice, have often resulted in obscuring the richness and freedom of the pardon which Christ Himself declared. Not infrequently men have turned away from the proffered pardon, bewildered and repelled by the framework of doctrine which seems to have been obtruded between the Soul and God. The living and winning power of God has been lost in an artificial scheme of abstractions. The Righteousness of the Law has been elaborately built up as a barrier against pardon, with a view of producing a real repentance; and then this difficulty has been removed by a theory of Substitution, as if Christ by His death satisfied the law, and so made pardon possible. Such attempts to explain a truth that is beyond our comprehension appeal rather to a tedious logic than to the deeper elements in our nature. And when doubt begins to question even the logic of the situation, the whole framework will hang, discredited, and out of gear, a positive check to the message it was once designed to convey. There are many souls that remain unpardoned, not because the pardon of God would be incredible or undesired, but because that cumbersome and unintelligible mechanism seems to stand as a lifeless obstruction to the advances of the Divine Love. We are not concerned just now with inquiring into the origin or use of such doctrinal systems. But, for souls in the bewilderment which has just been described, what hope and joy may lie in a reversion to the teaching of Jesus!

It is impossible to imagine anything more unembarrassed, more direct, more untechnical, than His appeal to the conscience and the heart of men. He appears to be entirely unconcerned about any system. It is true, as I think we shall see, that words of His imply an Atonement, a vicarious sacrifice for sin which He had come to offer. But never in His teaching does there occur a hint that to understand this mysterious transaction, or to hold a correct view of its processes, was a condition to be interposed between a repentant sinner, and a pardoning God. His word rather was, *the Son of Man has power on earth to forgive sins.* And while He required faith in Himself as a condition of exercising His powers, never did He mention any other condition, except the one on which He frequently dilated, that if a man would be forgiven he must forgive his fellow men.

Whatever terms are, in the thought of God, necessary to be imposed, in order that men may receive the pardon of sin, Jesus keeps them in the background, and meanwhile offers a free and unconditional pardon to every one that repents. His word is like a two-edged sword, revealing and condemning sin. At His clear and faultless goodness the conscience trembles like a guilty thing afraid. But He has so ordered it that no penitent soul can ever look fairly at Him without marking an outstretched hand, and hearing a voice of supreme compassion: *Thy sins be forgiven thee; go and sin no more.*

RIGHTEOUSNESS

Matt. v. 20.

I WONDER if to any of you has ever come an experience of this sort. Steeped in the theological notions in the midst of which you were born, have you, in reading the words of Jesus, ever felt uneasy, from a suspicion—never uttered or breathed of course—that they are not exactly orthodox? One theological Scotchwoman is reported to have said frankly that she did not care much for the discourses of Jesus because there was too much *morality* in them; by which she meant, not that they taught counsels of perfection, but that they seemed to attach salvation to good works in a way repudiated by the Westminster Confession.

The term "good works" has a sinister sound to evangelical ears. We usually feel that an explanation is necessary. If righteousness is needed in order to enter heaven, it is an *imputed* righteousness only, the righteousness of Jesus, and not our own.

Certainly the discourses of Jesus betray no trace of this doctrine. To suppose Him saying "My righteousness shall be accepted instead of yours" would be to render meaningless the most significant of all His utterances, that collection of sayings which we call the Sermon on the Mount. Throughout that sermon He speaks in the plainest and simplest way about a righteousness which consists in actually doing the will of the Father. To introduce the idea of His doing the righteous deeds for us would rob the whole argument of its application.

When a certain lawyer asked what he should do to inherit eternal life, Jesus did not make the answer which would naturally rise to the lips of Churchmen or Evangelicals to-day, but He inquired how he read what was written in the law; and when this very exceptional scribe replied in language like that of Jesus Himself, " Thou shalt love the Lord thy God .... and thy neighbour as thyself," Jesus said, *Thou hast answered right; this do and thou shalt live*.[1] In the same way, when a rich man addressed the same question to Him, Jesus replied by quoting the five commandments of the tables which bear upon our dealings with our fellow-men, and when further pressed added another, *Go sell whatsoever thou hast and give to the poor.*[2] And, as if to show that these were not isolated cases, He on one occasion laid down the broad general principle, *Whosoever shall do the will of God, the same is my brother, and sister and mother.*[3]

All this is very unorthodox according to the form which the Christian faith has frequently assumed among us. Nor does there seem any way of maintaining the current form of doctrine, except that which has been adopted—viz., to put the teaching of

[1] Luke x. 28.   [2] Mark x. 21.   [3] Mark iii. 35.

Jesus into the background and to devise plausible methods of explaining it away. And yet intrinsically, as we shall see, Jesus is far from contradicting Paul's doctrine of "the righteousness which is by faith." Between the master and the great apostle there is no collision. But Paul's writings are peculiarly easy to wrest,[1] and it cannot be denied that many worthy people, who suppose that they are advocating Paul's views, contradict the teaching of Jesus.

We cannot therefore be too decisive in marking that Jesus demands a real righteousness as the condition of entering into the kingdom of heaven, a righteousness which differs from that of the Jewish law only in being more inward, more intrinsic, more searching and absolute, a righteousness which in one place He does not hesitate to compare with that of God Himself. *Ye shall be perfect as your heavenly Father is perfect.*[2] The forgiveness which He offers to men—which we shall see He purchases for men—is free. But as He knows what is in men and searches the intentions of the heart, He only grants forgiveness to those who will make it the starting-point of a new life, to those—*i.e.*, who repent according to Shakspeare's definition of repentance—
> Heart sorrow and a clear life ensuing.

Thus, with the teaching of Jesus before us, and adopting His tests, we may be perfectly sure that forgiveness has not been given, and that the sense

---

[1] 2 Pet. iii. 16. [2] Matt. v. 48.

of forgiveness is simply a delusion of the deceitful heart, where the result is not the type of conduct and character which Jesus Himself prescribes. The principle He enunciates, *By their fruits ye shall know them*, applies to our self estimate as well as to the estimation which others form of us.

From all this it will be evident that the place of the Sermon on the Mount in the Gospel literature is not accidental. Necessarily the first task which the Master must take in hand would be to show in detail what is meant by Righteousness in the kingdom of God, and what manner of men consequently they must be who would *see life*. By a set design, which is accurately represented in the traditional arrangement of the materials of which our Gospels are composed, Jesus began by promulgating a law. Over against the righteousness of the Scribes and Pharisees, which was of an elaborate and conscientious, but not of a penetrating or inspiring, kind, He set—not by any means a doctrine of imputed righteousness—but a sketch of what a faultless righteousness would be which proceeded from the heart, and from a right inward relation with God. The character there depicted has met with general and sincere admiration. Seldom has it been slighted except by those who have theological systems which are at variance with the teaching of Jesus to maintain. The precepts of this law are very familiar to us all. And it is when He has passed them all in review that Jesus, with an impressive emphasis which no human language could surpass, declaring that *He that doeth the will of my Father in heaven shall enter into the kingdom of heaven,* utters a warning which, one would have thought, might have terrified those who deliberately set His teaching aside, *Many will say to me in that day, Lord, Lord, did we not prophesy by thy name, and by thy name cast out devils, and by thy name do many mighty works? And then will I profess unto them, I never knew you; depart from me, ye that work iniquity,* or, as the words imply, *ye that violate the Law,*[1] this new law of the Sermon on the Mount. And then *every one which heareth these words of mine and doeth them* is likened to a man whose house is solidly built, and *every one that heareth these words of mine and doeth them not* is likened to the man whose house comes about his ears with the rising of the flood and the downrush of the storm.

It would not be easy for any human language to express more clearly that the actual fulfilment of this searching series of moral injunctions is the condition of entering the kingdom. Nor can we see how Jesus could more deliberately have *excluded* the notions which have played so large a part in modern theology. But all this teaching of the Master Himself, different schools of religious thought have managed to make of none effect by their traditions. Evangelical teaching has followed a course so eccentric that at last it makes the teaching of Jesus seem unorthodox. It has come to such a pass that the Law of the New Covenant has been nowhere so discredited as in the house of His friends. As against His express words, *every one that heareth these*

---

[1] Matt. vii. 23, οἱ ἐργαζόμενοι τὴν ἀνομίαν.

words of mine and doeth them, a Christian lyric has been composed to the effect—

Doing is a deadly thing, doing ends in death.

If we come to ask what explanation they would give who have thus contrived to exactly reverse the word of their Lord, we get the answer, which has already been hinted at, that they are following the doctrine of St. Paul. " He gave us the apple," they say, " and we did eat." How indignant Paul would be at this suggestion, as if he, and not Christ, had been crucified for us ! What could be more evidently fallacious than to set Paul against his Master, whose slightest word was law to him. Personally I am persuaded that St. Paul, rightly understood, and put in his due subordination to the teaching of his Lord and ours, does not contradict Jesus. As this study proceeds we shall come quite naturally to the meeting-point, where the thought of the servant dovetails with that of his Master. But while there is any apparent collision, while to an imperfectly trained spiritual sense Paul seems to teach one doctrine and our Lord another, it is of vast importance that we should unhesitatingly give the preference to our Lord. The Sermon on the Mount comes before the Epistles of St. Paul, and must interpret them. Nothing could be more misleading than to use the Pauline Epistles to discredit the Sermon on the Mount. The result of a shallow and ignorant play upon words may easily be to make Paul explain the Teaching of Jesus *away*.

But we are touching now on a sin of the Church,

rather than a sin of inexpert and amateur theologians. It is not the individual that has buried the teaching of the Gospels under the metaphysics of the Epistles. That is the work of the Fathers, the authoritative Teachers of the Church, the Church itself. Indeed, with sorrow and shame we must as Churchmen confess that we have committed a sin against Christ. We have repeated the offence which Judah committed when the Book of the Law was lost in some dusty and cobwebbed chamber of the Temple. We need a new Josiah who will bring out from its hiding the first grand Law of the kingdom of heaven, the Law of the Sermon on the Mount, which lies covered and practically lost under the piles of ecclesiastical decisions, and under the burden of a traditional exegesis.

As this Law is read in our hearing—oh that we had ears to hear; oh that our ears were not dull and deaf with age-long prejudice!—as we study this Law, we are exceedingly filled with confusion. There is hardly a part of our practice or our creed, hardly an institution in the Church or in the State, which does not betray a departure from the faultless Law. So startling is the contrast, that a great prelate of the English Church ventured to say openly that the Law was a counsel of perfection and could not be realised in practice. To this has it come even in the most enlightened part of Christendom. But we must firmly insist: "To the law and to the testimony, if they speak not according to this word surely there is no morning for them."[1] The morning will break

[1] Isaiah viii. 20.

upon Christendom when we take the Sermon on the Mount seriously and practically as our law of life.

Now we will look at this Law of the kingdom as a whole. It is essential to look at it as a whole. For unlike all other laws, its precepts are not divisible. The Law is one. We are lost if we lose ourselves in detail. Let us fairly contemplate these two vital characteristics of the Law as a whole.

First, it is directed from first to last against ritualism, against the tendency to exalt tradition, against the accumulated authority of an ecclesiastical system which supersedes the immediate authority of God. The righteousness of the Scribes and Pharisees, the conception of religion which finds its expression in a series of outward observances, the mode of judging conduct by that which meets the eye of men and not by that which meets the eye of God —these are the things which come under condemnation. It can therefore occasion small wonder that the Church, in resuscitating all these features of a bygone system, has sought to repress the teaching of Jesus ; or that in England, when increasingly the popular religion leans on the example of pre-Christian Judaism, and when those ideas of Temple and Priesthood and Altar, which Jesus came to supersede, are made the essence of Christianity, the teaching of Jesus is ingeniously explained away. In the Church the stress is laid on things which have no place in the teaching of Jesus at all. He attaches no virtue to church-going. He makes no distinction between clergy and laity. He says nothing about sacred buildings, vestments, external ordinances, as the means of grace. All these things belong to another order of ideas. With Him the whole stress is laid on such matters as, being reconciled with your brother before you draw near to worship,[1] or, to use His own contrast with the elaborate prescriptions of earthly religions, on *judgment and the love of God*.[2] His favourite quotation from the Scriptures is not some description of the worship in the Tabernacle or the Temple, but a word from the prophets to the effect that what God wants from men is not sacrifices but Mercy.

Mercy! Think of that beautiful word. How merciless Churches and dogmas are! Yet how can we catch the spirit of His teaching while we think that our sacrifices, our Churches, our dogmas, are more important than mercy? He flamed into wrath against those who fasted and made long prayers, and wore religious vestments, and yet overlooked *judgment and the love of God.*[2] How scathing He was to those who kept the Sabbath, or made gifts to the church, and advanced these religious deeds as a plea for neglecting some service of love and pity to man!

Second. But if the first broad feature of His Law is antagonism to a lifeless ritual, the second is His rejection of Casuistry in moral conduct. With clear insight, and a convincing simplicity, which in any one else we should call genius, He penetrates the thousand and one precepts of the Scribes, and comes to the root of all right conduct. In one thought of inexhaustible import He supersedes, not

---
[1] Matt. v 24.   [2] Luke xi. 42.

only the Judaism which was before Him, but all the complicated and confusing systems of Jesuits and Canonists, that have come after him. Musty volumes and illegible parchments shrivel up in the flame of His zeal. He brings us to the one perennial source of religion and goodness in the twofold precept: *thou shalt love the Lord thy God with all thy heart, and with all thy soul, and with all thy mind, and with all thy strength. And, thou shalt love thy neighbour as thyself.*[1]

All the breaches of the moral law, murder, adultery, divorce, swearing, retaliation, and indeed all human actions, are referred to this one principle. You will not escape here on quibbles and legal technicalities. There are no formularies which human chicanery may twist or evade. Everything is tried at once by the essential test of Love, love to God, love to man. This goes to the foundation of the matter. Here everything is at once proved, good or bad, of what sort it is. Whatever comes from a fervent love to God, and an equal love to men, is good, though it may seem misguided, blundering, and ineffectual. All the deeds of apparent worth, working out in useful results, gaining the applause of men, are yet bad if they do not proceed from this twofold love. Not only hate, but egotism, is ruinous to religion, and from God's standpoint, to morality.

When all is thus simplified we may yet have questions to put. For example, Who is my neighbour? His answer is, Every one whom you can help

[1] Mark xii. 30, 31.

is your neighbour, stranger and Samaritan no less than friend and Jew. Or we may ask, What form must my love to my neighbour take? His answer is, *All things whatsoever ye would that men should do unto you, even so do ye also unto them.*[1] But what particularly shall we do to them? For a brief answer this: Give and forgive. The world says, Get. The Master says, Give. *When thou makest a feast, bid the poor, the maimed, the lame, the blind; and thou shalt be blessed, because they have not wherewith to recompense thee.*[2] If you have money, employ it to make friends who will be able to receive you in the heavenly mansions.[3] Again, the world says, Stand on your rights, retaliate an injury. The Master says, *Resist not evil.* Forgive the brother that has sinned against you, not seven times only, but as often as he sins.[4] And never judge men. Be faithful in rebuke, but never cease to love. Be careful too not to throw obstacles in your brother's way.

In a word, love to our neighbour is a humble, unselfish, tender, untiring beneficence to every one that comes within our reach.

Or we may ask, What does He understand by love to the Father, the strenuous and complete love which His words describe? The answer is given in the prayer which the children of God are to address to their Father. It is the humble and reverent devotion which places the hallow-

---

[1] Matt. vii. 12. [2] Luke xiv. 14. [3] Luke xvi. 9.
[4] Matt. xviii. 22. The seventy times seven is evidently an indefinite number.

ing of the Father's name and the coming of His kingdom before all personal desires. It is the trustful confidence in His perfect goodness, His love which anticipates and supplies all our needs. It is the sincere and heartfelt subjection of other interests to His. His great foe, Mammon, is dethroned. Goods, friends, relatives, are all subordinated to the Father's will. It is God first, and the rest by comparison nowhere.

And yet this exclusiveness of love to God is not, in the thought of Jesus, exclusive at all. God includes all. In this absorbing devotion to God, and in this alone, all objects of affection recover their worth—yes, even self, which otherwise would be lost, is restored.[1] Like a water-plant which grows in the ooze of the river-bed but only flowers when it gets above the surface into the upper air, we are so made that until we get above ourselves, above our surroundings, and penetrate victoriously into the love of God, there is no blossom or flower, no right love for men, no wholesome occupation with the things of sense and time. Until we are employed in Him, we stand all the day idle.[2]

Thus *the second commandment which is like unto it* grows out of the first. Disappointment is in store for those who put the second before the first. A human heart is not large enough to love the neighbour until it has been expanded by the love of God. Love is a great achievement, which makes demands on heart and soul and mind and strength, that is, on

---

[1] Matt. xvi. 26.   [2] Matt. xx. 6.

everything which goes to make up a man. It is achieved only by an active exercise towards the source of love, God Himself. When the tendrils of this plant have all been wrapped about God, the plant acquires a miraculous expansiveness and can reach out to men on every side.

Love God, and you will love men, is the way in which Jesus understands the Old Law and frames the New. Know your love to God by the growth of your love to men, is His test and criterion of inward religion, nor does He obscurely intimate that until a soul is thus developed into its full power of selfless love, it is and must be a lost soul.

This then, in its startling directness and simplicity, was the New Law. It did not so much abrogate the Old Law as fulfil it. Yet the Old was bound to pass when the New was once understood. For here was the strong wine of the kingdom which could not be put into the old bottles. No ecclesiastical forms had, or have, been discovered which could contain or express this thrilling truth—for it is the truth which forms the *nexus* of the universe and binds all created things and all righteous wills about the throne of God. Here was the new Temple which could only rise when the external Temple of marble and gold had been razed in the dust. The Church has greatly diverged from the teaching of the Lord—but has she improved upon it? Bent on putting the new wine into old bottles she has lost both. Determined to rebuild the Temple and to magnify her gorgeous buildings and her ceremonials of outward show, she has only succeeded in producing a petrified religion. Scandalised at the lowly mount on which the Sermon was delivered, she has crept back to Sinai, readopted the stone tables of the Law, the Tabernacle, the Altar and the Priest. And where is her Lord's idea of righteousness; what place does it hold in her practice, or even in her teaching? It is to her a heterodoxy—a counsel of perfection—a bundle of extravagant precepts, to be decently explained away.

But again we must repeat that His Law holds, His testimony cannot be antiquated: to the Law and to the Testimony; if they speak not according to this word surely there is no morning for them.

SALVATION

LUKE xix. 9.

TO utter the Law of the kingdom, if that were all, would do little towards saving men. As that Law is more inward and more exacting than the Law of Moses, it would of itself suggest only a more divine despair, a desire working like a passion, and a disappointment cruel as death. A high ideal does not necessarily carry with it an enabling power; and its presence, unless it is realised, must be a condemnation. Jesus Himself was often conscious of this, and said that it was better for those who had never heard, than for those who had heard and disobeyed.

The Kiung-Tsze, or *Princely Scholar*, of Confucius is a noble and attractive picture of what a Chinaman should be, but there does not seem to be in the life of Chinamen even a tendency to realise the ideal. And if there has been some effective striving of at least a few souls in Christendom to realise the Sermon on the Mount, it has been because Jesus had something else than a mere law of righteousness to declare.

So beautiful is that Law, so intrinsically attractive; and so perplexing is the comparative neglect which it has met with at the hands of Christians; that it can cause no wonder if some have been tempted to confine the teaching of Jesus to the Sermon on the Mount, and to propound this fair ideal as the means of saving the world. But that kind of Socinianism has been foredoomed to failure, not only because the Law is so difficult (more difficult even than that of Moses, which yet no one ever fully kept), but also for this still more intrinsic reason, that Jesus Himself does not allow us to remain within these arbitrary limitations of His teaching. If we receive from His lips the flawless Law, there is no reason why we should not receive from His lips another announcement—viz., the announcement of Salvation.

Through His teaching from beginning to end rings a glad message, the good news of a power that is able to save. The doctrine of righteousness, indispensable as it is, does not stand by itself; but like a precious gem is set in a ring of gold by which it can be bound to the finger. The ring of gold is the doctrine of grace. Jesus depicts His Father, the Eternal God, in the infinitely attractive hues of saving love. He represents Him as the Father who waits in His palace, expectant and welcoming, for the return of His prodigal children. But He goes farther than this. Like a shepherd, who sets out to recover the helpless and silly sheep that has wandered, God is seen coming to seek His lost. Jesus, in expatiating on His own intimate relation with the Father, recognises Himself and His errand on earth, as the expression of the Father's touching anxiety to rescue and to win sinful men. *The Son of Man came to seek and to save that which was lost.*[1] Every one will immediately acknowledge that this line of thought and feeling underlies all that Jesus says and does. It is impossible to read many paragraphs of any one of the Gospels—if our ears are not too familiar with the words to notice what they imply—without feeling that the presence of Jesus in the world has, to Himself, this saving significance. A chance reader who had no prejudice would never think that He was living for any other purpose than to save men.

It results from this peculiarity of thought and feeling in Jesus that the message which He took from the lips of John the Baptist, *Repent, for the kingdom of heaven is at hand,* acquired at once a new meaning. John intended a threat, Jesus intended a promise. From John the words meant: Escape for your life; the Judgment approaches, and the Judge comes with the awful winnowing fan to separate the chaff from the wheat. From Jesus, as all the Gospel shows, the same words mean: Change your purpose, misguided children of men; for your Father's arms are open to receive His lost ones and to draw them to His heart.

Jesus comes writing the tables of His new and blessed law, not on stone, with thunders and tempests and threats, and the terror of possible failure, but on human hearts with winsome gentleness, with a heart-moving sorrow for sin, and with a great enabling power. He has a royal road to hearts. If the new

[1] (Matt. xviii. 11.) Luke xv. 3; xix. 10.

law is exacting, the new Lawgiver has a power which Moses never claimed. There is no fear of a high demand, if He who demands approaches us with means of fulfilling it which He is ready to impart.[1]

To say that this doctrine was new is to say but little. It was so miraculously new and unexpected that we can safely say, the history of religions furnishes us with no parallel. Ingenuity has found in the scattered religious utterances of the world isolated sentences of the Sermon on the Mount— not the articulated whole in its completeness and cogency, but fragments which may in a sense detract from its originality. But no ingenuity has found any parallel to this which is the distinctive feature of the teaching of Jesus. No other teacher, in propounding a supreme law of righteous conduct, ever proposed himself as the means, always at the side of the believer, by which the law can be fulfilled. The law came by Moses, possibly, but grace and truth by Jesus Christ.

But we must defer to the next section the precise mode in which Jesus offers Himself as a Saviour. For the present we have to turn back and inquire what He means by salvation, when He says to a man: *To-day is salvation come to this house.* The meaning of Saviour must be determined by the content of the term salvation. In the words and thought of Jesus salvation is this: It begins in the seeking and the saving love of God, anticipating all; which can only be compared to a feast[2] with tables

---

[1] Hence that of St. Augustine: *da quod jubes, jube quod vis.*
[2] Luke xiv. 16.

spread and servants going out into the streets and lanes to invite all and every to come in and to partake It is a feast of fat things, a banquet of great joy. Thus, being very desirable, above all other possessions it is like a treasure or a pearl of price,[1] which, when one lights on it, one will endeavour to secure at all costs. Yet it is so free, a gift of so unconditional and unpurchasable a kind, that one can in no wise buy it, or receive it in any other way than as a present from God: *whosoever will not receive the kingdom of God as a little child shall in no wise enter therein.*[2] But suppose a man will come at the invitation to the feast, suppose he will receive the gift in a childlike way, suppose the window in the heart flies back for the light and love of God, the anticipatory and seeking love of God, to flow in, yes, suppose the man allows in his heart the least communion with that marvellous love; then a wonderful thing happens. A process immediately begins which may be compared with the yeast working in the dough, or with a seed, which, if it has got fairly embedded in the soil, will push and grow, until it pierces the dark earth, and springs up exultant to bear leaf and flower and fruit—a great harvest, thirty, sixty, a hundred fold.

Yes, if but the process begins, if but the contact takes place, if the grace of God effects an entrance, the progress is startling. It is illustrated by the familiar fact that to him that has, is given. If a man has money, money begets money; it grows upon him more and more even while he sleeps; it rolls

[1] Matt. xiii. 46. [2] Mark x. 15.

up in glittering piles until it hems him in, afflicts, torments, and possibly overwhelms him. Every one is eager to give presents to the rich; the poorest will lend to him; the most churlish will do him a favour. It is not a fact to rejoice in; it is a dark and even sickening fact in the kingdom of Mammon. But Jesus does not hesitate to borrow illustrations from these base things with which we are all familiar. And the fact which on the material side is so offensive, and so discreditable to our human nature, turned to the spiritual side, is full of bright and beautiful encouragement. Let a man make but the faintest response to the saving love of God in his heart, and more love streams in through the narrow chink. Let a seed get in at all, and it will grow. This golden coin of the kingdom increases at a compound interest. All the ministers of grace are eager to give to this openhearted recipient. Contact with God leads to converse, and converse to communion, and communion to that new and diviner indwelling, which was described as the sonship of God. The embryo passes to the birth. It is as if a new soul were born. Grace is not withheld but is given in good measure, pressed down and running over. Little by little the precepts of the new law become intelligible and practicable. The beatitudes fulfil themselves. All things are possible to him that believeth. Deep and firm the foundations are struck into the rock; and the fair, stedfast mansion begins to rise.

But while we may thus in general terms characterise the idea of salvation, gathering together the teaching of many rare and forcible images, it is possible to trace out the process with even more detail, and in a way which makes it more personal to the individual soul. Though He avoided here, as everywhere, anything like a systematic statement which might seem to reduce the work of God to a stereotyped order; and though it was always His method to reject that kind of treatment in which theologians and preachers have delighted; yet there are three stages, not sharply defined, but rather melting into one another, three moments, as philosophy might call them, in the progress of individual salvation, which, without putting any constraint upon His thought, we may distinguish and discuss. There is THE CALL, CONVERSION, and ADOPTION. The terms, or their equivalents, are His own.

I. The Call is illustrated by the striking stories already referred to, of the kingly banquet, in which the guests are invited, but make excuses and refuse to come. Then the invitation is extended to all, and yet not to all, because the invitation is valid only when it is received in a certain way, or rather perhaps it should be said, the invitation passes by like the wind unless the soul is in a receptive state.

For Jesus has His own doctrine of Calling and Election, not very like that which Augustine, Calvin, and Jonathan Edwards compiled out of the letters of St. Paul, and their own hearts, nor yet altogether that which has been substituted in Christendom today. Indeed, between the doctrine of Jesus on this subject, and the doctrine of the schools, there is all the difference that there is between the free song of birds and the shriek of a steam whistle. With Jesus the whole thought plays within the circle of human freedom and the sacred exercise of the will; appealing to those delicate and subtle possibilities which exist in every human heart. He invites a response, and encourages the outstretching of a hand, the heaving of a sigh, the hunger and the thirst after righteousness. The Augustinian doctrine, on the other hand, begins by practically denying the main fact—viz., the human will, and ends, if it be pushed to its legitimate conclusion, in the complete suppression of those ethical elements in religion which to Jesus are all-important.

He *came not to call the righteous but sinners;*[1] as a physician does not visit those that are whole, but the sick. That is, in a word, His doctrine of the Call. There is a voice which goes out with the utmost freedom to mankind, inviting outcasts, publicans and sinners, the mourners, the self-distrustful, those who beat on their breasts with the sigh of contrition, to come. The Call naturally makes no impression on the self-satisfied, the superior persons who need no repentance—to use His gravely ironical phrase—and who thank God that they are not as other men. Thus the Call is to all who will accept it. But, sorrowful fact of the perverted will and the blinded spiritual sense, it seems that only a few have even the slightest desire or can acknowledge the least feeling of need!

Nothing hinders Jesus from making the Call world-

[1] Mark ii. 17.

wide; but something in the human heart prevents it from taking universal effect.

And as there is this limitation in the Calling, so there is a further limitation, or perhaps the same limitation occurring at a later stage, in the Election. A guest appears to accept the invitation and comes to the banquet, but has on no wedding-garment. He is there quite out of place. Or to fall back on another image, the seed has fallen into a soil which seems to receive, but actually chokes it. The human heart may not respond to divine grace, may be in the mood that cavils and presumes. Some dark movement of the will may reject the inner meaning of the word, and set up a deadly opposition to the course which conscience dictates. Though for a moment the soul appears to respond, and comes readily along with the company that gather in the festal hall, it is entirely out of harmony with all that is going on, it has no inward relation with God;[1] the main initial petitions, *hallowed be thy name, thy kingdom come*, have no meaning for it. Self-interested, base, perverse, it belongs to the outer darkness. Malicious, bitter, revengeful, it has its natural part in wailing and gnashing of teeth. Thus it comes to pass, and no one says it with deeper or more yearning sorrow than Jesus, that while *many are called, few are chosen*.[2]

To call is within the power of the supreme will, and He calls every one. To be chosen depends on these little, futile, darkened human wills, and but few will accept the call. There is no narrowness or

---

[1] Matt. xxii. 11.   [2] Matt. xx. 16; xxii. 14.

limitation in the love of God. He makes His sun to rise upon the good and bad. He calls to Himself all the souls of men. He chooses all who will be chosen, all who make it possible by a readiness to conform to the inward conditions of light and love and truth, which make up the kingdom of heaven. But some, many, at present even as it seems most, make it impossible, choosing the broad way. T… are not serious. They would be … enter heaven as it shapes itself to the… But the real heaven they have no… appropriate garment for the feas… 'teousness of the new law, but this th… no r to put on. St. Augustine confe… conversion he prayed, but inwa… answer to the prayer, for salvation fro… The sins were sweet, deliverance was … toilsome way. That is an experience w… soul that is candid in self-examination will… stand. But they who, sincere, eager, and humble, respond to the saving love, they who, so far as they at present can comprehend, desire wholly the pure will of God, they who will take up the cross and follow their Lord; these are the *Elect*.[1] They do not respond because they are the elect; they are the elect because they respond. These are the violent who take the kingdom of heaven by storm, souls smitten with the desire of holiness and the vision of God, who will count all loss that they may gain Him. Their *names are written in heaven*.[2] In their tender susceptibility to the heavenly love, in

---

[1] Mentioned in Matt. xxiv. 24.   [2] Luke x. 20.

their whole-hearted and gathering surrender to the divine will, they begin, even from the early days of their election, to become labourers in their Lord's harvest,[1] seeking and saving that which is lost.

II. But we have anticipated a little, because, as was hinted, the three stages of salvation intermingle. We turn back to the idea of Conversion. When a man is called and chosen by virtue of this inner ... Father's saving love, this—which is ... of repentance and believing in the good n... accompanied by immediate forgiveness; f ... accepted and realised constitutes a... the co... —*i.e.*, a genuine inward change at ... heart and life, a turning to God, not ... resulting in the creation of a right ... which is the soil and the root of all ... d actions. *Except ye be converted and ...tle children ye shall in no wise enter into ...om of heaven.*[3] *When thou art converted, st...ngthen thy brethren.*[4]

St. Paul uses different words to express the same truth; where Jesus speaks simply of forgiveness and turning to God, St. Paul employs language which is almost technical, language which cannot be understood without the intervention of theology; he speaks of faith and justification by faith. The Church, to which theology has sometimes been dearer than religion, has preferred the words of Paul to those of Jesus. But the value of the words of Jesus is that it is impossible to give them a

---

[1] Matt. ix. 35-38.   [2] Mark i. 15.
[3] Matt. xviii. 3.   [4] Luke xxii. 32.

technical meaning; out of them no *systems* of theology can be constructed. They are direct and unencumbered; they do not savour of the schools, but well up, like living streams which flow from the everlasting hills. Consequently everything appears much simpler, though it may be much profounder, in His lips. The words of the beatitudes, or almost any of His lucid, heaven-revealing words, will excite an aspiration God-wards. The soul breathes the prayer, *God be merciful to me a sinner*—the prayer of His suggestion. A childlike faith springs up in the heart towards Jesus. And He says quite simply, *Thy faith hath saved thee: thy sins be forgiven thee; go in peace; sin no more.* With treatment so direct and powerful we become as *one of these little ones that believe on Him*.[1] It is no slight to the great apostle to say that even he, with all his powers of thought and expression, " never spake like this man."

III. It is on this Call and Conversion that, according to Jesus, *sonship to God*, or as the apostles call it, adoption follows.

It is to be observed that He does not sanction the confusing notion which spreads the fatherhood of God so wide that it becomes a mere synonym for creatorship. No one can be more explicit than He in asserting that ideally—*i.e.*, in idea or intention— all men are children of God. But as He, from His union with the Father, attaches an infinite meaning to the relation of Father and Son, He can hardly regard men in their rebellious, sinful and prodigal

[1] Mark ix. 42.

state as children of God in the real sense at all. The prodigal only reaches his father's heart, only in the real sense possesses a father, when he awakes to the humiliating discovery, *I am no more worthy to be called thy son.* While a man, among the swine-troughs, is blandly confident of the fatherhood of God, and his own accepted and discovered sonship, he is, in the view of Jesus, as it were, not a son. God may be his Father; he is not God's son. We have to *become sons of God* by an inward change, by a new birth, by a spiritual affinity and ethical assimilation to the Father. But directly that sorrowful and humble cry issues from the awakened heart, and the resolution is taken, *I will arise and go to my Father*, the goal is already in sight, the Father runs to meet the child. This is the view of Jesus, and as a practical moral force, it is evidently far more efficacious than the spurious charity which robs fatherhood and sonship of all ethical significance.

There is a glorious goal to reach, a dazzling possession, the title deeds of which Jesus is prepared to put into our hands. Beyond the little gate of forgiveness, rises the steep, exhilarating path of sanctification, which the children of God are to climb, until, the ridge of death for ever passed, they shall become in a full final sense, but half understood here, *sons of God, being sons of the resurrection*.[1]

A soul called, forgiven, changed, laid like a lost lamb on the shoulder of the Good Shepherd, to use that simplest, most exquisite of images,[2] responding,

---

[1] Luke xx. 36. [2] Luke xv. 5.

as is but natural, with a passionate surrender to the love which forgave,[1] the lost child addresses himself as a pilgrim to the way which leads back to his father's home.

A twofold thought occupies the mind of the returning one, the *rights* and the *duties* of sonship. Jesus has expounded in word, and fully illustrated by example, the extent of these. The rights are summed up in the second half of the Lord's Prayer, daily bread, continued forgiveness, deliverance from sin, the open-hearted communion with God, the surrender of all earthly care. The duties are: to claim these rights, to pray always and not to faint, to forgive, to love, to watch against temptation, to work in the vineyard; in a word, to live by the law of the kingdom, for which power is ever given in the present grace of the King.

Such is the nature, the manner, and progress of human salvation according to the Teaching of Jesus.

[1] Luke vii. 47.

THE MEANS OF SALVATION

MATT. xxvi. 28.

WE have examined the idea of salvation as Jesus presented it to men, an offer of free grace for all to accept who will. But we were obliged to defer for a moment the consideration of that personal agency by which alone it could be effected. That He from first to last is identified with the salvation of men can scarcely be denied, but what is His own specific teaching about the relation between the salvation brought and Himself who brought it?

This most fascinating question is now before us.

A flood of light is shed on His teaching by the recognition, which has only been made in quite recent times, that *there was a development in it.* As He grew in wisdom and stature from childhood; as His mission was gradually apprehended and accepted; so the narrative of the earlier Gospels gives decided hints, that after His work was distinctly conceived and vigorously commenced the means by which it could be realised were by orderly degrees unveiled before His eyes.

If all that He ultimately taught was clear and

complete to Him from the beginning, we are certainly landed in much confusion. If, for example, He had seen at once the significance of His own sacrificial death as the means of salvation, how could He have said to the palsied man, *Thy sins be forgiven thee*,[1] without any reference to Himself or to His sufferings-? But light breaks in upon the subject if we allow that while from the first He knew in His own heart the fulness and freedom of the Father's forgiveness, He only arrived by experience at the discovery that the sole condition of securing it to men lay in His own unspeakable suffering and death.

There is a story of the Old Testament which might have been designed to convey this thought in a figure. It is the story of Isaac, the resigned and loving son, who climbed the hill with his father for a sacrifice, saying: "Here is the wood and the fire, but where is the lamb?" In the same manner Jesus, with a lowly and watchful obedience, moved along the way which was appointed for Him by His Father, aware that there was a work for Him to do, never deviating for a moment from the path. But at a certain point the cross came in view, and He saw that He must be a victim; and "greatly amazed and sore troubled" He began to speak of the death which He should accomplish at Jerusalem.

At the first, in the buoyant confidence of truth, and the convincing charm of the kingdom and the heavenly fatherhood, He uttered His sublime thoughts as if He expected men to accept them

[1] Matt. ix. 5.

gladly. He was too occupied with the Father and the kingdom to speak of Himself. His own person hardly came into consideration. His attention seemed to be called to His position in relation to the truth which He taught by the animosity which was excited in the hearts of the rulers of the people. He was driven to fall back on His inward authority. And at last, as that animosity developed into murderous hate, He began to settle it with Himself that He must die, and that a world which was so eager to kill its Saviour could not be saved except by its Saviour's death.

In the fourth Gospel, which we are at present reserving for separate study, everything is regarded from the standpoint of the teaching long ago completed; and if we had only that Gospel, we should know nothing of this development in our Lord's human mind. But the Synoptics not only suggest, they require it. Until we recognise the fact, their records seem to be contradictory. When we recognise it we are drawn into a closer sympathy than ever with Him who in all points, except that of sin, shared our nature.

We have, therefore, to notice three stages in His exposition of the means of salvation. He never had to retract or even to modify what He said, but each thought was merged in the next as the rings of a tree's growth are included and retained in the thickening stem. What He employed at the beginning as the means of salvation remains permanently valid, though if it had remained alone it would have been ineffectual. It passed on to a more powerful mode, which in its turn prepared the way for the most powerful of all.

We fix our eyes on the *Word*, the *Person*, and the *Cross*. The word precedes the person, and the person prepares for the cross. The beginning would not have availed without the end; the end could not have been reached without the beginning and the stage that came between.

And if our records require us to follow out the means of salvation as they were gradually matured in the mind of Jesus, we have our reward; for in this way everything connects · itself with God's recognised method in nature and history. The analogy of human life, and the unfolding of its meaning with the advance of years, and the faithful use of experience, comes to our aid in understanding the most important of all human lives, and the most decisive of all events that ever happened upon the stage of history, or in the processes of this habitable globe.

1. The means of salvation in the first instance Jesus sought in the *Word* which He spoke to men, that utterance of invisible truth which welled out of His own pure consciousness. The words of a man's mouth are as deep waters, a wellspring of wisdom, a flowing brook.[1] This proverbial saying applied in a unique degree to one whose inner nature was united with God as that of Jesus was. Up to the end Jesus attached a remarkable significance to His Word, as we can see from the saying in the fourth Gospel, that His disciples were clean by the word which He

[1] Prov. xviii. 4.

had spoken to them.¹ But at the beginning it would seem that He thought of Himself as the utterer of the Word exclusively. This is implied by the first assertion of His mission in the Synagogue of Nazareth : *The spirit of the Lord is upon me, because He anointed me to preach good tidings to the poor. He hath sent me to proclaim release to the captives, and recovering of sight to the blind, to set at liberty them that are bruised, to proclaim the acceptable year of the Lord.*² Here He thought of Himself as the preacher, and even the release, the recovery of sight, and the restoration which He was to bring, would come in the form of a proclamation, as the result of the uttered word. The answer, which He gave at the beginning of His ministry, to John's puzzled inquiry, whether He were Messiah, carries with it the same idea : *Go your way and tell John the things that ye do hear and see : the blind receive their sight, and the lame walk, the lepers are cleansed, and the deaf hear, and the dead are raised up, and the poor have good tidings preached to them.*³

Here, it is true, the word was accompanied with power, or, as the wondering people would say, *with miracles*. But nothing is more remarkable in the teaching of Jesus than His mode of treating these miracles. To Him the word was everything, and the miracle quite secondary. Indeed, the miracles only applied to those who received the word. When men demanded miracles as a sign, He refused them with a grieved indignation.⁴ Or if sign there

---

¹ John xv. 3.   ² Luke iv. 18.
³ Matt. xi 5.   ⁴ Mark viii. 12.

was, it should be only a reference to the remarkable preaching of Jonah, which turned the Ninevites to repentance.[1] The word was the sign. They who perceived no miracle in the marvellous message of the kingdom and in the limpid truths of the new law, should not have their curiosity gratified by miracles which could be of no possible use to them. And yet He was quite aware that to seeing eyes the powers He exercised were a necessary accompaniment of the truth that He uttered: *If I by the spirit of God cast out devils, then is the kingdom of God come upon you.*[2] His only concern is to maintain that the message itself is of far more importance than the signs and wonders which are sure to follow it.

Thus the fullest illustration of this earlier method, and of the stage at which He regarded the word as the means of salvation, apart from any personal operations of His own, is the Parable of the Sower.[3] In that parable, according to His own interpretation, He Himself is simply the sower, the agent through whom the seed is cast upon the soil. The seed, on the other hand, contains the potency in itself, and its fruitfulness is determined by the receptivity of the soil. Whoever allowed the word to enter his heart and grow, would bear fruit; but if the word were plucked up, withered or choked, there would be no result.

Compare this detachment of the sower from the seed, and this assurance that the seed in virtue of

---

[1] Luke xi. 29. [2] Matt. xii. 28.
[3] Matt. xiii. 18; Mark iv. 14.

its inherent power would accomplish the work, with the later idea of Jesus presenting Himself as the bread of life to be eaten; and it is impossible to deny that there was a remarkable progress in His conception of the means by which salvation could be effected.

It is through noticing only this germinal form of His teaching about the means of salvation, and through not recognising the progress in His thought which is reflected in the Gospels, that some plausibility has been given to the belief that Jesus was nothing but a teacher, proclaiming a truth which had an intrinsic power in it irrespective of the Person who proclaimed it. Jesus undoubtedly in the first stage of His ministry spoke of Himself in that way. There was an exquisite self-abandonment in Him. In the glowing enthusiasm of those early days, when the word He had to speak seemed self-evident, and there could be no doubt but that all who heard would receive it, He was not anxious to obtrude Himself on the mind of His hearers. It was the seed, not the sower, that seemed to Him all important.

It would almost seem as if Jesus, in His complete innocence, and guileless inexperience of human sin, in spite of the temptation which followed His baptism, did not realise that the world could not be won merely by preaching, or by the declaration of soul-subduing truth. Innocence never at first suspects, and on the first suspicion is unable to credit, the dark mystery of evil in human life. A soul that loves truth cannot conceive how souls should prefer a lie. And Jesus, in the faithful fulfilment of His work had to discover—as His words were twisted and misrepresented by evil hearers, and His works were ascribed to Beelzebub—that a pitiless foe was in possession of this world which He had come to save, a strong man armed, whom He would have to overcome in the stern grapple of death.[1]

2. The very remarkable passage, Matthew xi. 25-30, which is there closely connected with the unbelief and opposition His word had met with in Galilee, marks distinctly the second, reflective stage of His teaching about the means of effecting salvation : *I thank thee, O Father, Lord of heaven and earth, that thou didst hide these things from the wise and understanding, and didst reveal them unto babes. . . . . All things have been delivered unto me of my Father; and no one knoweth the Son save the Father, neither doth any know the Father save the Son, and he to whomsoever the Son willeth to reveal Him.*

As time went on He found it impossible to ignore the significance of His own person. He found, in comparing Himself with other men, that He alone stood in that intimate relation to the Father. The conclusion was inevitable that He by His very nature was a mediator, the one living link between the heavenly Father and His erring, travailing, and heavy-laden children. The fact must have lain in His being from the commencement of His life. But it was, apparently, realised in consciousness at a certain point, *at that season.*[2]

So meek and lowly of heart was He, so alien to

[1] Mark iii. 27, Matt. xii. 29, Luke xi. 21. [2] Matt. xi. 25.

His nature was any kind of self-assertion, that He was slow to recognise or to announce this supremely significant fact. And, it would seem, this native modesty and delicacy of a perfect soul made Him always more inclined to hint at it, and trust to the apprehension of His hearers, than to enforce it, in what might have appeared a spirit of egotism.

But it was necessary to put constraint upon Himself. Just as in a crisis of danger it will sometimes happen that a timid and retiring woman suddenly starts to the front, and, with unsuspected force of will and salutary self-assertion taking the command, and leading more turbulent spirits in quiescent obedience, saves the situation, so—using the imperfect human image—in the crisis of the world's salvation, Jesus, the meek and lowly one, found it necessary suddenly to assert Himself, and for the world's good, unflinchingly to bring out His unique nature and calling.

There is no psychological study more fascinating than this human soul, which, without resigning for a moment its position of incomparable humility, makes claims, never made by men even in the extravagance of boasting or the exaltation of despotic power. *He that receiveth you,* He said, *receiveth me, and he that receiveth me, receiveth Him that sent me*[1]—*i.e.*, God himself. And, *every one that shall confess me before men him shall the Son of man also confess before the angels of God.*[2] Or, *he that is not with me is against me, and he that gathereth not with me scattereth.*[3] Or more startling still, *where*

---

[1] Matt. x. 40.   [2] Luke xii. 8.   [3] Matt. xii. 30.

two or three are gathered together in my name, there am I in the midst of them.[1]

Language of this kind, perfectly simple, natural, and modest as it is, implies a personal claim which is quite unlike anything we find elsewhere in human experience. He could not, in a false modesty, shirk His great position. Like a general of an army, in whom the refusal of self-assertion would become a crime, He was unable, without imperilling the salvation of the world, to withhold the astounding truth. He was, nor could He fail to recognise it, the personal conqueror of the power of evil, entering the strong man's house and binding him. He could not disguise that on a personal relation with Himself must therefore depend every man's share in the conquest, every man's triumphant reconciliation with God. He spoke with a calm conviction of His victory: *I saw Satan fall as lightning from heaven.*[2] It would have been cruelty to men, a base desertion of which He was incapable, if He had shrunk from presenting His own power, which He was able to communicate to them: *I have given you power to tread on scorpions and serpents, and all the powers of the enemy, and nothing shall in any wise hurt you.*[3]

Truth required, the very word He preached required Him to take this position. The claim was absolutely quiet and absolutely firm. It was free from ostentation; it was also free from hesitation. And when once that point was reached, His ministry asumed the form, *Come unto me.*[4] The word of the

[1] Matt. xviii. 20.
[2] Luke x. 18.
[3] Luke x. 19.
[4] See Matt. xi. 28.

teacher became secondary, introductory, to the teacher of the word; and the attention of the hearers, arrested by words such as never man spake, was rapidly centred on Him who spake them. The image of the sower passed into that of a shepherd seeking his sheep.

3. But a third and final stage in the unveiling to Himself of the means by which salvation should be effected, came—and the point is very distinctly marked in the Synoptic Gospels—at that moment, when, in conflict with the rulers of the Jews and their invisible ruler, Jesus perceived that He would have to die, and to die not in the way that is the common lot of men, but in a way which was invested with a peculiar significance, a way which would demand an unexampled endurance and suffering. Only by death could He accomplish that which He had prepared by living. This was the conviction which settled in His mind, so that He began to conceive His death as the supreme means by which He would secure salvation for the world.

We are permitted to obtain some glimpses of the way in which this truth dawned upon His consciousness, and of the agitation which it caused in His spirit. When He began to teach His disciples that the Son of man must suffer many things, and be killed—when such language became open and unambiguous[1]—it not only caused a shock to His disciples, but beyond all question it worked upon His own soul in a manner which can only be explained by the issue involved in His death: *I have a baptism*

[1] Mark viii. 31–32.

to be baptised with, and how am I straitened till it be accomplished?[1] So powerfully did the thought affect Him that it betrayed itself in His appearance, and as He approached the altar of His sacrifice they who saw Him were struck with amazement and fear.[2] Whether the meaning and precise bearings of this baptism of death assumed a distinct shape in His mind, our records do not enable us to determine. There it seems like a dark, mysterious fact, big with doom, which breaks upon Him like the sound of angry seas heard in the night. Yet, it is evident, He distinctly believed that His approaching death was not only an incident of His life work, but an integral part of His mode of saving men. For one chance saying of His has been preserved, which, as a sign of His habitual thought, is more impressive than a deliberate elaboration of doctrine : *the Son of Man came not to be ministered unto but to minister and to give His life a ransom for many.*[3] From one point of view this saying provokes, rather than satisfies, curiosity. For it is left indeterminate to whom the ransom is paid, and how precisely the release is effected. But as an indication of His own thought about His death its importance cannot be exaggerated. It was a common saying in Hebrew that a man *sold* himself, or was *sold* to do evil.[4] And more than once Jesus adopted a form of speech which implied that man was bound prisoner to Satan. How far this was mere metaphor, or a

---

[1] Luke xii. 50.   [2] Mark x. 32.   [3] Matt. xx. 28; Mark x. 45.
[4] See 1 Kings xxi. 20, 25 ; 1 Macc. i. 15 : " They forsook the covenant, and were sold to do mischief."

literal description of fact, who can say? But clearly men were, in His view, held in a bondage of sin from which they were powerless to release themselves because they were in no position to pay the ransom which would set them free. And His death, He saw, sufficed to pay that uncalculated price, and so to purchase the deliverance of men.

At the Supper, on the eve of His departure, this idea was not explained but carried into the heart of the Church, never to depart, by an impressive and tender symbolism. It does not seem to be always recognised that a few pregnant words on a great occasion may be of more significance than the diffuse and flowing talk of a lifetime, when no stress breaks up the deeper fountains of feeling or redeems language from its tendency to extravagance. Thus many have been unwilling to attach their due importance to these few brief sayings uttered under the shadow of the impending cross. The historical associations and the sensitized perceptions of those who sat at meat are overlooked, and the words torn from their surroundings are taken in a cold and disconnected bareness of suggestion. But remember that the blood of the Paschal Lamb spared the Israelites in Egypt from the visitation of the destroying angel. And remember that the most moving of all the prophets, Jeremiah, had spoken beforehand of the new covenant which was to be written on the heart of the people. And then consider what was implied by saying, *This is my blood of the New Covenant which is shed for many*.[1] And see if that addition is

[1] Mark xiv. 24.

not implicit in the whole situation : *unto remission of sins*.[1]

Certainly He must have felt that His blood shed —*i.e.*, His approaching death—was about to secure a deliverance from sin, as the blood of the Paschal Lamb saved the Israelites from slaughter. And by connecting the Covenant with the blood He must have meant that the new and inward cleansing, foretold by Jeremiah, was to be accomplished by the death He was preparing to undergo. If the details are left indistinct, as it must be acknowledged that they are, it is hardly conceivable how He could have more impressively indicated that His death was the supreme means by which men could be saved ; nor could He have shown more directly that its virtue was to be appropriated by an individual act of faith than He did by saying, *Take eat,* and *drink ye all of this,* and *this do in remembrance of me.*

Here was a mystery which He never attempted to explain ; nor have the explanations offered since the time of the Apostles thrown any appreciable light upon it. But His own action and His own words leave us no alternative : when we would state the means by which salvation is effected, according to the teaching of Jesus, we must dwell not only on His word and work, not only on the mediation of His unique Person, but also on His death, the sacrifice offered upon the cross for the sins of the world, and assimilated by the powerful faith in Him which finds its best symbol in the *eating and drinking* of His flesh and blood.

[1] Matt. xxvi. 28.

Looking back we are bound to recognise that the free proclamation of Pardon with which He began was all along implicitly conditioned by that prevailing sacrifice with which He ended.

The salvation which was depicted in the first sermon could only be achieved by the means depicted in this filial action.

THE CHURCH

Matt. xvi. 18; xviii. 17.

THE world has heard more than enough of what the Church says about Jesus, but how little has it heard, as yet, of what Jesus says about the Church! It has been the hard lot of multitudes to know Him only through the Church, and thus never to get the criterion by which the Church itself is to be judged. For them the Church is Christianity, and Christ is but a part of the Church. The Church looms large, a venerable and beautiful building, the growth of many ages, with crumbling images of the saints, and storied windows of far-off and half-forgotten things, intricate, attractive, bewildering, subduing, a sum of impressions rich in antique associations, half Christian and half pagan, half worldly and half heavenly, at least worldly enough to make worldlings at home in it. And in some niche or other of the great edifice is Christ, a conventional Christ; in the Virgin's arms it may be, or swung on a colossal crucifix from the chancel roof. Perhaps a great painter has made an altar-piece, or a fresco. Perhaps a great composer has breathed a suggestion of Him into the pipes of the high-built organ. Perhaps a preacher, in the midst of much talk about Sacraments, Saints, Fasts, and Feasts of the Church, confession, decoration, contribution, mentions with a distant reverence, and a customary inclination of the head, "Our blessed Lord."

Consider, a great part of Christendom has as yet hardly looked upon Jesus, or heard Him speak. "Look at the Church; hear the Church," has been the Gospel for the ages.

It is therefore a new idea to sit at His feet and ask Him what He teaches about this institution which, for good or evil, has practically superseded Him. Has He in any way anticipated history and spoken with prophetic censure and praise about the Church which claims Him as founder? Yes, He has.

What has to be said on this subject is revolutionary. His teaching reads like a set indictment against the historic Church. Men, heartsick and disappointed, have passed scathing judgments on the Church in each successive age. Jesus has anticipated them all. From the first He announced what He would do with the unfaithful steward; He would cut him off and appoint him his portion with the hypocrites.

Let us be careful how we approach His teaching on this subject. If you come with a foregone conclusion, if you are a special pleader for the Church as we know it, you may read into His words the abuses of Christendom. Every error has managed to connect itself with some words of His, so that tracking back the error we seem to run up into His words as the source. Remembering this, we have to ask simply what He meant—not, can His words be twisted into a sanction of this or that practice, but what was the first intention of His words? If His edicts were designed to correct the corruptions of history, it is a transparent fallacy to justify history by corrupting His words.

He is quit of all blame for the abominations which have discredited the Church. The things which have been the stumbling-blocks to honest souls have no kind of authority in His teaching. They are ancient, it is true, but not quite ancient enough. They are not apostolic, but sub-apostolic. It would be grossly unfair to charge upon St. Francis the evils which developed in the Franciscan order within a century after his death, because we are aware how an astute Vatican exploited and reversed the founder's beautiful ideas. It is equally unfair to credit Jesus with the iniquities of the Church, the greed, the ambition, the materialism, the cruelty of priests, the idolatry of sacraments, the supple untruthfulness of Jesuits. For, the world, Judaism, the empire, Paganism, exploited His ideas. In the lifetime of His contemporaries the mystery of evil began to work. Ignatius, the little child, it is said, whom He set in the midst as an example to His disciples, already in the next generation, we must believe if his epistles are genuine, introduced the arch heresy. Before a second century had passed, Tertullian, Irenæus and Cyprian had admitted the ideas which were gradually to reverse the teaching of Jesus.

But here lay the wonder of God's wisdom. The very men who were unconsciously drifting from Jesus preserved His teaching to be their judge and correction. These three Gospels remain, a source of truth, pure and undefiled, when the waters which flowed from them at the first became foul. We are perpetually carried back to the Jesus who lived and spoke among men. And as, with these Gospels in our hands, we study simply what He said about the Church, the whole worldly structure of the ages, stained with stupidity, unreason, insolence, ambition and avarice, passes away like the baseless fabric of a dream, and we see the Church, His Church as He conceived it, like a fair bride, chased from the altar into the wilderness, pursuing her gentle and holy course down the centuries, attracting slight notice from men but close attention from heaven, persecuted, despised, forsaken, yet cherished, glorified, victorious. Sometimes for a day or a night she tarries in some pretentious hostel which has assumed her name, finding the door-keeper for the time charitable and Christlike. But for the most part she has been, and must be, in the wilderness, until the cry rings through the midnight, " Behold the Bridegroom cometh." I am conscious how difficult it is for those who judge according to appearance, and have no clear idea of the forces which ultimately shape and determine events, to recognise this astounding paradox; but the study we now essay should make it clear that what Jesus means by His Church has only an occasional and fitful connection with what is known in history as the Church, the

Church which is the theme of ecclesiastical historians.

Let us with an unbiassed mind examine the two passages in which the word *Church*[1] occurs on the lips of Jesus, and summon to our memory the numerous sayings of His, which refer to the idea without mentioning the name.

First, there is the promise addressed to Peter in Matthew xvi. 18. There came a point in the ministry of Jesus, after He had expounded the nature of the kingdom of heaven, and shown how its establishment on earth was connected with His own person, when one solitary human being understood Him and believed. It was a fateful crisis in history. Stand for a moment by that little group of men at Cæsarea Philippi, and listen to that heartfelt avowal in answer to the question of Jesus, *Whom say ye that I am?* "Thou art the Christ," said one "the Son of the living God."[2] In all this world which He had come to save, here was one simple and open mind that recognised Him, only one. Crowding multitudes with noisy acclamations had greeted Him and offered Him ostentatious fealty. But they were of no avail. On such outward and unspiritual foundations no spiritual and inward structure could be reared. But here was one man inwardly con-

---

[1] It is well known to scholars that these two passages are not of unquestioned authenticity. But believing them myself to be authentic, and wishing to examine the teaching just as it has come down to us, I have not thought it worth while to pause to vindicate the passages.

[2] May I be allowed to refer the reader to my own *Cartoons of St. Mark*, p. 161, for this scene?

vinced, one man bound to him by a personal passion of loyalty and love. In that one man He saw the potency of everything; in that believing and confessing soul He already foresaw His Church. That one soul was at present His whole Church. The name of the man was Rock. And with a beautiful allusion to his name, Jesus said, "On this Rock will I build my Church."

One man alone at present; but in the one was the promise of all that should be. And therefore He hastens to give to the representative man the promises which will hold for those whom he represents. The gates of the invisible world shall not prevail against that building which he sees rising ideally into heaven. This confessor, and all confessors who shall follow, are immortal. To this one man Jesus proceeds to entrust the powers which the community of His believers would necessarily possess. Using a phrase familiar at the time, according to which the Rabbis were said to "bind" or to "loose" when they declared anything to be in accordance with, or contrary to, the Law, He buoyantly declares: "Thou, believing soul, trusting in me, shalt have power so to lay down the laws of life and conduct on earth, that thy decisions shall be ratified in heaven." This frank and passionate confession of Christ has introduced the soul at once into the kingdom of heaven, and established a correspondence between what is done by it here and what passes in the spiritual council chamber. Here then is a rock on which the kingdom of heaven can, even on earth, be established, a rock for the

THE CHURCH

moment precisely coextensive with this one man, the rock, Peter.

Second. That we have got essentially the right meaning of this famous passage becomes clearer when we turn to the other occasion on which Jesus used the word *Church* (Matt. xviii. 15-20). We are here moved from Cæsarea Philippi to Capernaum. There the Church consisted for the present of one. Here it is already "two or three." More than one had now made the significant confession. There would be an assembly, however small, of those who believed; the rock would not be a single stone, but a building of lively stones fitted together, as Peter himself says.[1] It was time, therefore, to sketch in a general way what the relation of the members was to be.

And here observe, lest it should appear that the power to loose and bind had been committed to Peter as a personal prerogative, and not merely as the essential power entrusted to a believer as such, Jesus repeats to the company of believers the precise words which He had uttered to Peter when Peter was the sole believer.[2] And, lest there should be any foothold for the notion that He addressed those first few believers as an Order, which should have certain functions and prerogatives distinct from those of the community of believers, He proceeds to state in the most general and embracing terms what He means by the society, to which these powers are entrusted. He defines it as the assembly which is constituted by men gathered together in His name

---

[1] 1 Peter ii. 5.   [2] Matt. xviii. 18 and Matt. xvi. 19.

with the consequent personal presence of Himself in the midst.[1]

But as the community would thus be formed by a personal relation of each individual to Himself, the members could not be less than brothers. In a word it would be a brotherhood. Everything would depend on maintaining the brotherly feeling. If that were lost the spell would be broken, and the ties would be dissolved. A breach of brotherly love would be equivalent to a wrench of him who should be guilty of it from the person of Jesus. Accordingly, the primary endeavour of the society would be to preserve this unity of spirit, the bond of peace. If, therefore, one of the brotherhood has committed an offence against another, the injured one must at once strive to gain him by frank and affectionate remonstrance in private. If that fails he must ask two or three others of the community to come with him, to check the unfairness of a possible bias, and to widen the range of motives for reconciliation. If that fails, the whole brotherhood must be informed of the root of bitterness, the "little rift within the lute, which by-and-by would make the music mute." If the offending brother stands out against the representations of the whole brotherhood, he is by that very fact excluded from the brotherhood. Where the whole bond is love, the lack of love is excommunication. If this contumelious individual is not exorcised, and treated as a Gentile and a Publican, the brotherhood itself must quickly lapse into the mere dissolution of the Publican and Gentile world,

[1] Matt. xviii. 20.

the society of the Christless everywhere and at all times.

But while the free and spontaneous fellowship is maintained, each vitally related to Christ, Christ in the midst of all, the society has a power which surpasses all the combined powers of the world. It is the power of consentaneous prayer. What it asks shall be done for it by the Father which is in heaven.[1]

Brief then as these passages of the Church's foundation are, the idea is singularly clear. No language could define more simply and directly what Jesus means by the Church. The key to the idea is a personal belief in Him and a personal confession of His name. Such a belief and confession bring the admission of the kingdom of heaven into the soul. Receiving the kingdom of heaven as little children, these confessors become the sons of God, and therefore brothers. United with Him, Jesus Christ, they are drawn together in a spiritual community, and He is personally present with them. Their prayers prevail; their mutual discipline becomes the shaping of life; their decisions about what is permissible or not have a heavenly significance and a binding authority on the community.

It is a sweet and pure spiritual reality—the Church as Jesus conceives it—a gracious liberty of love, a mutual ministry, a common worship, an atmosphere of self-forgetfulness, humility and prayer. It is a creation of fire and dew, a kind of heavenly city coming down on the earth. It is on the earth but

[1] Matt. xviii. 19, 20.

quite unearthly. It can be bound in no buildings, defined by no formulæ, defiled by no abuses. All the earthly societies called Churches are immediately tested and tried by it. Touch them with this Ithuriel's spear, and their quality becomes manifest. Is the brotherhood there unbroken? Does love prevail? Is Jesus in the midst? Do they pray, and praying receive? Ah, this then is the Church. But are they full of mutual rivalries, hatreds and contempts? Have they no discipline of mutual ministry, no prevalent prayer, no test of the inward relation to Jesus? Then that may be the Church of Rome, or the Orthodox Church, or the Church of England, or an Independent Church, but it is not what Jesus Himself means by His Church at all.

But here is the most revolutionary feature in the thought of Jesus. In His Church a hierarchy is expressly forbidden. *Ye know that the rulers of the Gentiles lord it over them, and their great ones exercise authority over them. Not so shall it be among you.*[1] *Be not ye called Rabbi: for one is your teacher and all ye are brethren. And call no man your father on the earth; for one is your father, which is in heaven. Neither be ye called masters; for one is your master, even Christ.*[2]

We have heard it said that the Church is constituted by a hierarchy of priests. In this hierarchy each priest calls himself father, and the chief priests holy fathers in God, while at the head of them all is *the* Father, Papa, or Pope. We have seen in history these high functionaries lording it over the

[1] Matt. xx. 25. [2] Matt. xxiii. 8-10.

THE CHURCH

flock of Christ in a way which makes the authority of kings and the insolence of tyrants seem slight by comparison. We have heard the loud assumption that the common people cannot know the truth but must accept the teaching of the Church.

By all these things the Church has defined herself very distinctly and has succeeded in showing that she is not the Church of which Jesus spoke. In His Church there are no priests, and there is no clergy, except in the sense that the whole community of His loyal ones form a *clerus* and ministering priesthood in the world. Within its borders the only pre-eminence is that of sacrifice and service. The only exalted ones are those who are abased, those who spend and are spent, and are in the footsteps of the Lord *who came not to be ministered unto but to minister and to give His life a ransom for many*.[1]

Then, always on the assumption that the spiritual should be first, and indeed everything, He adopted two outward symbols to express the essential reality. They who believed in Him should be inwardly cleansed, therefore let them be outwardly baptised with water which should mark and define the spiritual fact. The society too of His confessors, living in intimate brotherly love, sustained continually by His imparted life, washed inwardly by the powerful operation of His sacrifice, should seek to express this divine reality by the repeated observance of the last meal which He ate with them on earth. For indeed it was His purpose not only to be in their midst, but to be in each one, as a bread on which

[1] Matt. xx. 28.

the soul could live, as a life-giving power which would contain the element of cleansing.

The word "sacrament" is none of His coining. The sacramental idea is the antithesis of His, who taught that nothing entering into the physical organism could affect the spiritual life.[1]

And now to throw together the ideas which complete His teaching about His Church: His confessors were to be a light in the world, a city on a hill. Each one of them was to be a sacrifice salted, as it were with fire,[2] the community was to be in the world as salt, saving the world from corruption. Each one was to be severe to himself but tender and affectionate to the rest. "What the soul is in the body that Christians are in the world," says that early Christian apology, the letter to Diognetus. The Church was not to obtrude *herself*, but to proclaim that supreme invisible kingdom of God. Each member was to be a fisher of men, going out to seek them, persuasively compelling the lost world to come in, proclaiming on the house-tops the message he had received in the ear.[3]

And as He despatched His messengers on this world-wide mission, His heart melted with solicitude and compassion over them. They would be like sheep among wolves; proclaiming the kingdom of peace they would be involved in weary strife.[4] They would have to glide through the world, wise as serpents, but harmless as doves.

He indulged them in no illusions. He did not

[1] Matt. xv. 17; Mark vii. 18. [2] Mark ix. 49.
[3] Matt. x. 27. [4] Luke x. 3, xii. 51, xxii. 35-37.

leave their weak faith to be shattered by unexpected corruptions, by huge hypocrisies, by the veiled enemy in the garment of light. He frankly foretold all. Among His wide-sown wheat an enemy would sow tares. False teachers would emerge—not like His own sheep among wolves—but wolves in sheep's clothing.[1] Even the loudest professors who had spoken and exorcised in His name would be rejected if their life did not accord with His demands.[2] From the first, therefore, He discouraged us from going by appearances and loud-swelling pretensions, and led us to fix our eyes on the consummation of this age, when the mysteries would be cleared; when His Church would be gathered, and the faithful would shine as the sun in the kingdom of His Father.[3]

Though therefore the Church in the lips of Jesus is very diverse from what is usually meant by the Church in the lips of men, it is sufficiently distinct, transparently simple, and undoubtedly attractive to the human heart in a way that the Church in the historical and human sense can scarcely be said to be.

[1] Matt. vii. 15–20. [2] Luke xiii. 26, 27. [3] Matt. xiii. 43.

THE JUDGMENT

MATT. xxiv. 36.

IF there is no task more important than that of understanding what Jesus Himself meant by His Church, there is none more solemn, and more heart-searching than that of studying what He taught about judgment. Questions about the Church always seem a little remote and impersonal. But judgment comes home to us. It is impossible to forget that we who inquire what it means, are they also who must be judged. Nor is the solemnity of the task lessened by the discovery of its difficulty. Though He said much on the subject, it was for the most part in parable or metaphor. Was His purpose to baffle carnal and curious minds? Did He leave His thought vague and awesome, intending to strike home to men of all kinds, to force inquiry, to make known the truth in proportion to the sincerity of the search, to secure the end that the truth discovered should not be flaunted in pride, but only applied to the serious practice of life?

Yet the difficulties of our task are not all of His making or permission. We shall do well perhaps to state clearly the hindrances which make it hard to distinctly frame His teaching on the subject.

Partly, as He expressly tells us, the matter was hidden from His own eyes, and known only to the Father. Unlike some exponents of prophecy whom we find in these days prepared to sketch the whole course of coming events with exact dates, as if they were admitted into the secret counsels of the Most High, Jesus confessed that on one important point at least knowledge was withheld from Him.

How that brief admission draws us to Him! No accurate mapping of the unknown future could be so reassuring. It is like a hand reached out to us in the darkness, as if He said: "Children, do I not know that the sorest sorrow of humanity is its ignorance about the future, its doom to walk in the bewildering mists, to light unawares on what is to be, to quit the hold of the life that is seen without a detailed assurance of the life that is to be? And do I not share this sorrow too with you? Be content, even I do not know when the goal of this world's history will be reached. My Father has not revealed it to me."

There are some who, to increase His glory, would hush this up or explain it away. They would strike down the gentle human hand held out to comfort us. "Thou art God," they say, "only God; though Thou tellest us Thyself that Thou art human, we will not believe Thee. Thy infallibility ceases where Thou tellest us that Thou art not infallible."[1] Such

---

[1] May I refer to Dr. Dale's striking remark that the heresies of Apollinaris and Eutyches survive in the ultra-orthodox view

a dogmatic view has not only rendered the Gospel narrative incredible, and encouraged the persistent attacks of scepticism; but it has deprived the Saviour's character and work of one of its most enduring charms. The Church continues to write apocryphal gospels for the supposed glory of Jesus. But it is not possible to increase the glory which shines from these authentic Gospels as they stand. It is this perfect frankness of Jesus, His clear truthful eyes, the lowly renunciation of all pretence, the ready confession of ignorance, that gives us our supreme confidence in Him. The charlatan delights in nothing so much as in boasting of a knowledge which cannot be brought to the proof. He who is very scrupulous in stating the limitations of his knowledge, as eager to state what he does not as what he does know, establishes at once a claim on our trust. Consequently nothing inclines us to believe all that He distinctly states about the judgment so much as this clear confession that there is one thing which He cannot tell. We acquire a conviction that nothing would induce Him to state what He did not know. No detail will be supplied from the resources of apocalyptic invention. Whenever we can clearly interpret the imagery, and find what He intrinsically means we shall know that the result may be unquestioningly accepted.

At the same time, a complete ignorance about the time when the final judgment should take place, might well throw an air of uncertainty about much

of the mental nature of Jesus in the present day ?—*Christian Doctrine*, pp. 54–59.

which would be said. At least with such a caution from His own lips, we must be prepared to acquiesce in ignorance about much which we should be well pleased to learn. We must allow the existence here of an initial difficulty which has not confronted us in any other branch of our inquiry.

But partly also the difficulties arise from another circumstance which is tolerably plain to a careful reader of the Gospels: the first hearers of the discourses on this subject were in some uncertainty about the connection of ideas. While the greater part of His teaching was of so lucid, or so epigrammatic a character that it lodged easily in the memory, and appears in different documents with only the slightest verbal changes; the passages which describe the final judgment betray by their blurred appearance marks of a primitive confusion.

In this chap. xxiv. of St. Matthew, for example, the forecast of the destruction of Jerusalem, which was to take place within that generation,[1] between thirty and forty years after Jesus spoke, is accompanied by the statement that, *immediately after the tribulation of those days*, shall occur the second coming of the Son of man, and the final judgment of the world. Here the facts known to us, who have survived by many centuries the catastrophe of

---

[1] Matt. xxiv. 34: That γενεά could mean the Jewish race is a harmonistic theory which I cannot even entertain. I assume that it means what in all Greek literature it always means—viz., the family existing at a given time, and, in a secondary sense, the time which such a family exists together, or, as we call it, a generation.

70 A.D., leave us but two alternatives. Either the evangelists have grouped the sayings of Jesus in a misleading order, or if Jesus uttered them as they now stand in this chapter, He fell into a great mistake.

Now in such an alternative few of us can hesitate for a moment. The evangelists appear in their writings as very artless and, outside their own subject, not specially well-informed men, who, when they attempt interpretations of the Master's sayings, not infrequently get wide of the mark. He, on the other hand, appears, even in these unskilled pages, as the most marvellous Being who ever opened His lips to teach mankind. Where He tells us frankly that He does not know a date we shall believe Him; but we shall be very slow to believe that He could have made so great a blunder, and have uttered it in so confident a way, as to say that *immediately after* the destruction of Jerusalem His second coming would take place, especially when this collocation is directly followed by the statement, *of that day and hour knoweth no one, not even the angels of heaven, neither the Son.*[1]

We may say, therefore, that we have here an internal proof of the fact that tradition had not accurately recorded His specific forecasts of the final judgment. There was an initial confusion between certain things He had said concerning the downfall of the temple and Jerusalem, and certain descriptions He had given of the Last Day, and the return of the Son of Man as the Judge of mankind.

[1] Matt. xxiv. 36.

Possibly this confusion was permitted in order to discourage from the outset the idle and demoralising efforts of those who attempt to describe the course of coming events. Certainly there could be no more striking rebuke to this unprofitable occupation than the fact that a prophecy put into the lips of Jesus, as we have supposed, by His first biographers was not fulfilled. That generation passed away and now sixty generations more, and yet *all these things* of v. 34 are not accomplished.

There are then two sources of difficulty which have to be constantly remembered, the limitation of the Lord's own knowledge on this subject, and a confusion which must have been present from the very first in the reports of His utterances touching the future.

And yet, when all allowance is made for these difficulties, His teaching on the two central and vital principles is perfectly clear and overwhelmingly convincing. He leaves no doubt on either point:

WHO WILL BE THE JUDGE,
WHAT WILL BE THE PRINCIPLE OF THE JUDGMENT.

Uncertainty rests, perhaps by design, on the time when the judgment will take place. There is no attempt to fix the point at which the fate of human beings becomes irreversible. Jesus, for instance, does not assume that the doom is fixed at the time of the body's dissolution. And to the question whether few or many should be saved, Jesus opposes a most direct refusal to give any answer.[1]

[1] Luke xiii. 23.

Let us try then to dismiss with the fewest possible words the doubtful questions, in order that we may concentrate our attention on the two points that are certain. And we observe at once that, true to its constant character, human nature delights to exercise itself with the very things which Jesus left uncertain, while it is very shy of meditating on those things which He presents to us with the clearness of day.

It will be enough if we convince ourselves by a brief survey that these uncertainties are absolute and designed.

1. *The Time of the Judgment.* In the examination before Caiaphas, Jesus said: *Henceforth ye shall see the Son of Man sitting at the right hand of power, and coming on the clouds of heaven.*[1] This remarkable announcement leaves us no option but to believe that His sitting on the right hand of power, and coming visibly on the clouds of heaven was an event which began there and then with His crucifixion and the following occurrences. It suggests that His coming is visible to those only who have eyes to see, and that they who do not see Him coming now will not be able ever to see Him coming, except by some decisive change in themselves.

2. The assumption made by the later Judaism,

---

[1] Matt. xxvi. 64, ἀπ'ἄρτι could not mean "hereafter." It definitely implies that the vision described began *from that time*. See Matt. xxiii. 39: "Ye shall not see me *henceforth* (ἀπ'ἄρτι) and John xiv. 7 "from now (ἀπ'ἄρτι) ye know me."

as well as by other religious systems, that immediately after death, the soul is carried before a judge and its final destiny there and then irreversibly fixed, is never distinctly affirmed by Jesus. If the Parable of Dives and Lazarus, which is only a parable, suggests it, the apologue of the sheep and the goats distinctly states that this decision is reached only when the Son of Man comes on the throne of His glory.[1] But, if we are to interpret Jesus by Himself rather than by Jewish and Pagan presuppositions, we should gather that death is an incident which may be ignored; the soul passes on into the next world precisely as it was in this, there to receive stripes many or few. He implies that sins may be forgiven in this world and the next.[2] And the whole course of His teaching suggests that the spiritual processes which are begun here must work themselves out to their legitimate conclusions of good or evil.

3. He observes a purposeful silence about the number of those who shall be saved. Indeed from His point of view the question would be misleading, because its underlying assumption was that everything was determined in this life.

And in addition to all these points of uncertainty it is to be observed that Jesus has a way of using the word *resurrection*, which shows how irrelevant many of the questions are with which we exercise our minds. By *resurrection* He does not mean the life beyond the grave, nor yet the resuscitation of the material body, but rather a completed life in the

[1] Matt. xxv. 31. [2] Matt. xii. 32.

living God. Hence He says: *They that are accounted worthy to attain to that world and the resurrection from the dead*[1] shall live a life emancipated from earthly conditions. He speaks of *the resurrection of the just*[2] as if to imply that in His sense of the word the unjust will not rise at all. And thus the sons of God attain to that condition, *being sons of the resurrection.*[3]

We have said enough to show that on many of the points about which the Church tries to be precise and dogmatic, Jesus prefers to be vague. Nay, may we not say that implicitly He has decided beforehand against some of the most confident conclusions at which dogmatic Christianity has arrived?

But now we may turn to those two certainties on which, as He left them indisputable, we cannot too emphatically insist.

First. Jesus Himself is the appointed Judge of men. It was no new idea that God should be the Judge. The Old Testament was full of it. But certainly here was a new and notable fact, that He had delegated the function of judgment to this Son of Man. *All things have been delivered unto me of my Father.* We may speedily establish the fact from His unequivocal utterances, and with equal ease we can follow out what is implied by it. *The Son of Man shall come in the glory of His Father, with His angels; and then shall He render unto every man according to his deeds.*[4] In the

---

[1] Luke xx. 35.   [2] Luke xiv. 14.
[3] Luke xx. 36.   [4] Matt. xvi. 27.

interpretation of the parable of the Wheat and the Tares, He says: *The Son of Man shall send forth His angels, and they shall gather out of His kingdom all things that cause stumbling, and them that do iniquity, and shall cast them into the furnace of fire.*[1] He declares in the plainest terms how He will Himself close the door on those who have made only a formal profession: *Then will I profess unto them I never knew you; depart from me, ye that work iniquity.*[2] He Himself, by a process which He describes in detail will separate between the sheep and the goats, and utter the doom of each.[3]

But these clear statements of the fact derive their significance from the particular meaning which He gives to the function of the Judge. It does not seem to be so much a verdict passed by one who has heard the evidence and sums it up impartially, as a sentence which results from the touchstone of His presence. He implies that He—partly the word He has spoken, partly the works He has done—but essentially He Himself is the standard by which men will be tried. In some of His sayings the idea of the Judge almost melts away, becomes an inappropriate image. There appears rather simply the gracious Saviour of men, the only one who could really save them, and for that reason the only one who can really judge them. He is there, not only in the last day, but now always in the course of human history, in our midst, willing to save all who will accept His call,

[1] Matt. xiii. 41. [2] Matt. vii. 23.
[3] Matt. xxv. 34, 41.

THE JUDGMENT

rejecting literally no one, but for that reason passing an unwilling verdict on those who will not come unto Him that they might have life. It seems to be in this sense that He regards His function of judgment as beginning from the time of His manifestation to men. And we almost gather that the scene of a judgment bar, and the dramatic division of all mankind into two classes at one moment, is sketched for the sake of pictorial representation to the multitude; but that what fills the mind of Jesus is that intrinsic determination of men's destiny by contact with Himself in the field of human experience. Following up this suggestion, which comes more from a study of His modes of thought than from an accumulation of particular utterances, we arrive at the idea that He is the appointed Judge of all mankind for this reason: at the long last, when the ultimate destiny of every human being will be determined, the one factor which will be decisive must be *the relation of each to Jesus.* Only the Christ-like will survive; every human element which is un-Christ-like must perish everlastingly. It is not the design of God that out of the human race anything should effect a lodgment in eternity which is out of Christ. Thus it can be no question of a formal profession of crying Lord, Lord, and recounting deeds done in His name. That is nothing to the point. It is all a question of inward resemblance to Christ.

Dante, with his poetic insight and the indignant justice which overruled all dogmatic conceptions, did not hesitate to put Popes in Hell. Augustine and the various theologies which have followed in his wake have readily consigned to torment all who were not of the elect. The Poet is much nearer to the thought of Jesus than the theologian. The idea that damnation is predetermined by the decree of the Omnipotent is devilish. But Dante has at least grasped the thought that the doom of men is fixed by intrinsic qualities. Arbitrary formulæ, outward professions, garb, cowl, tiara, do not come into consideration. But Dante was too far from the Teaching of Jesus Himself to see precisely what He meant.

From Him we get this grand and simple thought: to be like Him is everlasting life, resurrection, sonship to God. Whatever human being has received this seed of life into himself, and is so maintained and developed in a vital, spiritual union with Him, can never die. But on the other hand, human nature, which develops away from Him, chooses for itself a character which incurs the judgment, *Depart from me, I never knew you.* And that—even though it should be a whole soul thus permanently determined into hostility to Jesus—has no principle of life in it at all. It falls εἰς κόλασιν αἰώνιον, a phrase which can only be interpreted by the contrast of ζωὴν αἰώνιον.[1] To be in Christ is *life everlasting;* to be out of Christ is *punishment everlasting*—*i.e.*, a punishment which must last so long as the condition out of Christ lasts.

Second. But as we obtain a clear view of the sense

[1] Matt. xxv. 46.

in which Jesus is the judge, we are admitted at once into the principle which determines the judgment. We have several very precise utterances on the subject. He is always very careful to separate Himself from those who maintain that men will be judged by the opinions they have held, or by their external connection with a particular Church. It is hard to say which is farther from His thought, the churchman who tells the simple villager that every one who does not belong to the Church of England will be damned, or the doctrinaire who says that every one will be sent to hell who does not hold the correct views about Scripture, the Trinity, the Atonement, and so on. Jesus says sometimes: *By thy words thou shalt be justified, and by thy words thou shalt be condemned*,[1] because the words are an expression of the inner disposition of the heart. Or He says: *Not every one that saith unto me Lord, Lord, shall enter into the kingdom of heaven, but he that doeth the will of my Father which is in heaven.*[2] Or, He will *render to every man, according to his deeds.*[3] In the description of His judgment which enters most into detail, the decision turns upon loving ministry to others, given or withheld, which He regards as ministry to Him.[4] But no saying of His takes us nearer to the centre of the matter than: *Every one who shall confess me before men, him will I also confess before my Father which is in heaven. But whosoever shall deny me before men, him will I also deny before my Father*

---

[1] Matt. xii. 37.   [2] Matt. vii. 21.
[3] Matt. xvi. 27.   [4] Matt. xxv. 31, *et seq.*

which is in heaven.[1] In the light of the other sayings it is impossible to mistake what He means by confessing. It is the opposite of mere "professing." It is that manifestation of His reign, His power, His presence, which can only be made by a course of conduct in harmony with His will because directed by His personal control.

The teaching which has been offered to men on this subject has often had nothing but a verbal connection with the ideas of Jesus ; and it has sometimes been a refuge of lies which His word sweeps ruthlessly away.

"What creed do you hold? Do you belong to the true Church ? Are you baptized ?" Questions like these will not so much as be asked. But this, and this alone : "What art thou ? What through thy probation, or through the spiritual circles thou hast travelled, hast thou become ? Here is the eternal standard—Jesus, this pure and self-less heart, that sees God, this fountain of love and grace that blesses men, this happy, restful spirit in the bosom of the Father. What resemblance hast thou to Him ? What relation hast thou with Him ? Art thou such as He ? Art thou to the all-discerning eye discernible as such ? Has life been an utterance of Him, a deed of Him, a confession of Him, or the reverse ?"

The selfish, the loveless, the malicious, the untrue, have no part in Christ, but march for ever on the descending road, the broad, easy, tormenting road of Death ; torment for them ceases only with their

[1] Matt. x. 32, 33.

being. But have you a part in Christ; art thou His; hast thou His spirit; art thou growing to His stature? Then come thou blessed of the Father, and inherit the portion prepared for thee in Him.

Thus Jesus speaks, dealing always not with vague fictions and fancies, threats and hopes, but with truths and facts which cannot be reversed.

THE CROWN OF THE TEACHING.

JOHN xiv. 26.

WE have now traced the main outlines of the Teaching as it has been preserved in the three earliest evangelic records. We have not digressed into detail, nor have we indulged in discursive expansion. We have tried to get as complete a view as possible of the structure as a whole. This is what Jesus taught in the audience of the people, and—can we wonder?—"all the multitude was astonished at His teaching."[1]

But we can hardly follow out the teaching as it appears in the Synoptic Gospels without the conviction that what is there recorded implies more. If He said so much, how can we avoid a belief that He —at least on occasion, to some chosen hearers— enlarged and explained? Especially when His design obviously was to gather a few intimate friends to whom He could expound what the world was not able to receive, we instinctively feel that He must have unbosomed Himself to them; He must have spoken expressly without parables to them what in these *Memorabilia*, which we call the

[1] Mark xi. 18.

Synoptic Gospels, appears only in the form of hints, dark sayings, or symbols.

We may at least distinguish seven points on which the teaching in the Synoptics seems to be the pledge of fuller statements; nay, one might say, the keys surely would not have been given unless there were corresponding locks to open. As we study the Synoptics, and surrender ourselves to their charm, we cannot but say to ourselves: If we had been there in the private conferences when He drew the disciples apart to rest awhile, or left the scene of His labours for a sojourn in Decapolis; if we had been present with them in the silence and the shadow of the night, by the well, or on the sea; we should have heard the enlargement of these themes, the eager questions of awakened listeners, the explicit and ever-memorable answers of the Master.

The seven points which must have been elaborated are these:

1. The nature of that infinite Being whom Jesus called with so appropriating and intimate a confidence, My Father.

2. How in His own consciousness Jesus perceived Himself to be related to His Father.

3. Whence He had come: whether, like us, out of the nothingness and forgetfulness of birth, or from an antecedent existence.

4. What more explicitly might be the inner blessing of that salvation, the character and means of which He had expounded.

5. What would He mean by the invitation to

come unto Him when He should, in the natural course of events, be withdrawn from sight and touch by the impending death.

6. What would be the law and the development of the community which He was founding on earth by proclaiming the kingdom of heaven, the society to which sparingly He gave the name of Church.

7. Might we know anything more explicit of that which awaits us behind the hills of death?

He must have said much on these points which the Synoptics do not record. They present the springs of the arches, but do not follow them up into the groining of the roof. Would such a building be left roofless? And further, it needs hardly be said that a teaching so original and so profound, bound up too, as it evidently was, with His Person, not His earthly life only, but His death, and that after-presence which was already promised by the resurrection: *lo, I am with you always, even to the end of the world*,[1]—such a teaching was not to be grasped in a moment or by hearsay; it must have time to be fused and harmonised by a living experience, interpreted by reflection, connected by links of moral assimilation.

Essentially this was a doctrine which, as a merely formal code, might mean little or nothing; all would depend on the practical working of it. To enumerate its precepts, to learn its ideas, would be but an insignificant part of the whole. The first thing must be that there should be someone who would live it all, someone who through the long years would

[1] Matt. xxviii. 20.

make trial of its possibilities, test whether the doctrine was of God, translate thought into action, and show how the bright vision of that stainless life, and the tender seed of the doctrine, might be perpetuated when Jesus could be seen and heard no more. The teaching of Jesus was of a kind that could by no possibility be immediately recorded, for this reason, that its very essence must be the transfusion which would take place in the experience of a believing, surrendered, and developed soul.

In a word, a study of the Synoptic records gives rise of itself to a new demand. We want to know not only what a reporter might have heard on the hillside or in the precincts of the Temple, but also how the matter would present itself to one who occupied the position to which Jesus referred in the words—*to whomsoever the Son willeth to reveal Him*.[1]

Now these demands which beforehand we should inevitably make, these questions which we cannot but prefer, are met by that book which is certainly the most remarkable document in human literature, the Gospel according to St. John. We have, I trust, been impressed by the teaching as it occurs in the other three Gospels; but it is no disparagement to them to say that they would remain incomplete without the fourth. Indispensable as their witness is —nay the fourth without them would hang in the air, and appear unreal, unhistorical, the creation of a constructive imagination—they without it would remain like a building four-square, and well set on a sure foundation, but *lacking a roof*. The Teaching of

[1] Matt. xi. 27.

Jesus, and the biography of Jesus too, would remain a roofless structure, a house hardly habitable for the spirit of man, if we had not this mysterious and unique book, which is called John's Gospel. Here the teaching we have been trying to study assumes a new aspect; as if the fronds had unfolded into the full leaf, or as if the parts had been pieced together into an intelligible whole, this seems to be the completion of what went before. Here the words are fused and fashioned into the symmetrical unity which in the early records was presupposed but not expressed. Everything is translated from the language of a certain epoch, a certain country, a certain situation, into the language of all time and all places. The teaching is the same, but changed. The vocabulary is changed; the ideas are the same. It is the difference between the lesson which a child has learnt by rote, and can easily repeat on leaving school, and the lesson as it appears in the mature and practised experience of life.

But it is important for us to mark several of the phenomena of this book, which evidently is not meant to supersede the others, but fulfils the desirable purpose of completing and interpreting them.

First of all, St. John always presupposes the other three. If we cannot say with certainty that he had the Synoptic Gospels, as we have them, in his hands, yet it is plain that the tradition embodied in them was familiar to him, and the general contents of the narrative were so far taken for granted, that he does not attempt to repeat what in them has been well said. We are at liberty therefore to assume that the teaching of Jesus in St. John is to be explained, where necessary, by the teaching in the three.

Again, St. John has a superior knowledge of the framework and detail of the life, so that where the Synoptics give scattered and disconnected episodes, by no means agreeing even among themselves about the connection of certain passages, St. John moves along with a carefully marked chronological order. It must be observed, however, that he does not use this more accurate knowledge for the purpose of exhibiting the development in the teaching; a fact which we gather entirely from the three; but interpreting always the beginning by the end, he introduces the whole body of the teaching at the several occasions which his narrative embraces, with the effect that it appears as a uniform and compacted whole. Accordingly, while the fourth Gospel is the best of all for tracing the main course of events in the life, it is the least serviceable of all for fixing the date of any particular doctrine. As we have already seen, the teaching has in the writer's mind been so fused and harmonised by the experience of years that it presents itself to him no longer as the diary of the words of Jesus, but as the articulate and completed Word itself, the Word embodied in a human form.

Then, as to the authenticity of this unique document; there is an uncertainty which might be of design, as if men were not to have the assurance of this ripest truth of religious experience guaranteed by science, but only by faith. Hence extreme views are still taken about the authorship of the Gospel. But when faith has given us the cue, we observe a curiously subtle and convincing guarantee of genuineness in the notice of chapter xxi. 24, where some unknown witnesses attest that the disciple who leaned upon the breast of Jesus at the Supper was the author. The self-suppression which led him to withhold his name as unimportant—and the way in which he, at the same time conceals and obtrudes his personality, thrusting himself forward veiled as it were, is one of the most striking characteristics of the composition—this self-suppression is not permitted to discredit the value of the testimony as a first-hand witness. Even where doubt still lingers about John the Apostle being the author, a candid consideration of internal evidence convinces one that here is the direct evidence of one who saw and heard.

But another point is to be noted. Wendt has certainly succeeded in showing that the teaching of Jesus in the fourth Gospel is essentially identical with that in the other three. Misled by the variation of form, critics have from different points of view assumed that a totally new doctrine is introduced by St. John. They have attributed this to the free creation of a religious or philosophical speculation suggested by anything rather than the historical person and life of Jesus. These vagaries of criticism must be curbed by the discovery that so far from differing, the vital and fundamental elements in St. John's version of the teaching display the most remarkable identity with those in the Synoptics, an identity which is even emphasised by the variation of form and of terminology. As we are now about to see, the teaching in St. John is simply the teaching of the Synoptics clothed upon, and articulated, and so carried out to its completion. It is such an expression of the doctrines as might conceivably have been given by Jesus in the days of His flesh to a circle of sympathetic listeners; but much more strikingly it is such an interpretation of His words as would gradually dawn on a devout and believing soul, who, cherishing with a passionate regard all that He ever said or did, had endeavoured for many years to live it out in the way that He had Himself directed.

We have therefore in St. John not only some of the deeper and more inward thoughts of Jesus which did not find a place in the Synoptic tradition, but also a certain spiritual and experimental expansion of His thought which He Himself had mediated, not through His human lips in the days of the flesh, but through the operations of the Spirit promised and sent to those who believed.

But now we must consider for a moment the astounding *difference of form* in the fourth Gospel, to which allusion has been made. This difference might conceivably be in part explained by a difference in subject-matter. When the Master was speaking about the kingdom of heaven, and the new law of the kingdom for its citizens on earth, He might present His thought in picturesque parables and aphoristic sayings. While, on the other hand, such a mode of speech might become inappropriate when He wished to speak of the more inward things, eternal life rather than the kingdom of heaven, or the Son of God, rather than the Son of Man. It is quite intelligible that the crisp and pointed style of the Sermon on the Mount would be best for a description of the life, and the works, which would distinguish the children of the kingdom; but another and more mystical mode of speech would be required when it became necessary to explain how that life would be produced by faith in Himself, and how therefore to believe in Him would be to do the works of God.

In so wonderful a mind as that of Jesus, there should be no difficulty in allowing room for many modes of speech, and forms of teaching.

But that this does not account for the difference in St. John's Gospel must be admitted. For precisely the style which characterises the words of Jesus in that Gospel characterises also the narrative itself. Indeed this mark of style more than once makes it difficult to determine whether the evangelist is recording the words of Jesus, or proceeding with words of his own.[1] It is this fact which seems to place it beyond question that the writer and not Jesus is responsible for the form, and the precise wording of these discourses. The Gospel of John does not as a rule give us, as the Synoptics do, the exact words of Jesus, as it were stenographically recorded; but it gives us the teaching of Jesus remembered and treasured in substance, shaped in the mystical consciousness of one who had been

[1] See John iii. 16, &c.

revolving His ideas, and finding modes of expression for them through a period of half a century or more.

Yet let us not be misunderstood. The actual sayings of Jesus are there, unmistakable in their originality, shining like gems with more than earthly brilliance; but they are set in the silver framework of the disciple's thought. The disciple did not, indeed could not, have invented them; they are as high above him as the stars are above the lamp-lights of the city street. Nay, so far from inventing them, he was not always capable of understanding them. On two occasions he essays interpretations of the Master's words which are more than doubtful.[1] But while he records the imperishable expressions and thoughts of Jesus, he clothes them in a language, and places them in a connection, of his own.

The recognition of this last fact brings, it should be remembered, a relief to some of the difficulties which all of us must have felt in the Gospel of St. John. Occasionally the controversy between Jesus and the Jews gives an impression of wrangling which is little in the style of Jesus; and it is remarkable that the passage which offends worst in this particular, chapter viii., bears on its surface the proof that it is not a correct record, but a careless compilation. For at ver. 30 we are told that "as he spake these things many believed on Him"; and He proceeded to speak to those Jews who had believed on Him; and yet a few verses lower down, ver. 44, He is represented as saying to these believers, "Ye are of your father the devil; because

[1] John ii. 19-22, xii. 32, 33.

I say the truth ye believe me not." We could not have a more emphatic reminder that we are bound to allow for the interference, and the imperfections, of the biographer.

It is this manifestation of the earthen vessel containing the treasure that brings out the lustre of the treasure. The limitations and crudities of the writer are the proof that he could not have invented the thoughts which he attributes to Jesus; though they remind us that he has clothed them in a dress of his own. John is no doubt a striking personality; the Gospel and Epistles have a peculiar stamp; but his genius, and the unquestionable power of his writings, owe all their value, not to anything intrinsic in them, but to the remarkable manner in which they have conserved, fused, and interpreted the teaching of Jesus, and those more mystical parts of the teaching which the other records had lost or overlooked.

But let it not be thought that in saying this we are passing any reflection on the author to whom we owe so much. He himself observes more than once that the things which were said and done were not at the time intelligible even to the disciples, but became clear afterwards only on reflection, and by an inward illumination.[1] Indeed he finds authority in the words of Jesus for the method that he adopted, and those words are a further proof that we have rightly interpreted his method: *These things have I spoken unto you while yet abiding with you. But the Comforter, even the*

---

[1] John ii. 22, xii. 16, xiv. 26.

Holy Spirit, whom the Father will send in my name, He shall teach you all things, and bring to your remembrance all that I said unto you.[1] The teaching of Jesus in the fourth Gospel is not only what was spoken, while He was abiding with them; it is not only what was brought to their remembrance afterwards; it is also a fulfilment of that other part of the promise, *He shall teach you all things.* If one of the immediate circle of disciples who heard that promise had not attempted such a spiritual recollection, and enlargement of the teaching, this promise would have remained unfulfilled.

No shadow of deception is chargeable on the evangelist for this labour of love. When memory did not accurately distinguish between words actually spoken in those far-off years, and words breathed by the Spirit in the secret intercourse with the risen Lord, he would, as in the case just referred to,[2] leave it indeterminate whether he intended the language to be attributed to Jesus on that occasion, or only to the subsequent unfoldings of His spirit. From v. 19 in that passage, *the light has come into the world, and men loved darkness rather than the light, for their deeds were evil*, we should gather that the paragraph is the comment of John, and not the continuation of the discourse to Nicodemus. For in those words the evangelist seems to be looking back on the rejection of Jesus at the hands of men, which, when Jesus was addressing Nicodemus, had certainly not declared itself. And again and again the form of the language in the mouth of Jesus is more appropriate

[1] John xiv. 25, 26.   [2] John iii. 16–21.

to A.D. 90 than to A.D. 30. For instance the clause introduced into the great prayer, *and this is life eternal, that they should know Thee, the only true God, and Jesus Christ whom Thou hast sent*,[1] is from the use of the designation Jesus Christ, more like the comment of the disciple in after years, than the actual form in which Jesus would have addressed the Father in the days of His flesh.

But we must recognise that the evangelist wrote not only in good faith, but under the direction of the Spirit. All was, if not exactly what Jesus said in the years 30–33 A.D., yet exactly the utterance of Jesus as it sounded in the vital experience of "His own," not only in the year 90 A.D., but on and on until now; exactly as it will sound until His voice shall be heard again by human ears.

But if we may explain in this way the very striking differences between the fourth Gospel and the other three, differences which have led a large number of critics in modern times to reject the authenticity of St. John altogether; if we may in some such way as has been indicated maintain that we have here a trustworthy source for the genuine teaching of Jesus; and if we can offer, as we have proposed, some reasonable account of those features in the work which cause perplexity even to devout believers; we are justified in reaching a very decisive conclusion. This is not only one source, it is the most important source, of the teaching. Without casting any slur on the others, we must recognise that none of them can give us what this author

[1] John xvii. 3.

does. As Beyschlag says, "with all its freedom and subjectivity the fourth Gospel remains the most faithful image and memorial of Jesus that any man could produce." If it is not so verbally correct as the others, it is much truer. For which is the truer, a photograph or a portrait by a great master? The one, you say, must be correct, for it is the work of the light itself. Yes, but we all know that a creative artist can bring out much which is there, though the light itself does not detect it. Or, for that matter, which is truer, a reporter's verbatim account of a speech, compressed at his own discretion into a column or two, or the free reproduction of a sympathetic hearer, who has let the utterance sink into his mind and commingle with his thought, and then gives his impressions of it in his own way? In the first case there may not be a word or a sentence which did not come from the speaker's lips, and yet it may be a far less true account than is given in the second case, though scarcely a word, or at least not a sentence, is what the speaker said.

. The fourth Gospel demands from a student of the teaching an even closer and more meditative consideration than the other three; because the mere words count for little; learning by rote accomplishes nothing; it is necessary to get at the thoughts behind the words, and at the truth behind the thoughts. We must not for a moment overlook what it is that we are handling; unless we realise the extraordinary characteristics of the work, we are sure to blunder.

This is what comes before us: a disciple, the

beloved disciple, who heard all that others heard, and much more in secret which he alone, or he and a chosen circle, heard; one who passionately and tenderly received what he heard and made it his own; one who at the giving of the Spirit on the day of Pentecost, underwent that baptism of illumination and power, and then for many years, until all his contemporaries had passed away, wrought out the doctrine in the founding of churches, in the care of souls, in the service of the brethren, in the perpetual insistence on the central truth of religion; this disciple, before the mists of death fell upon his eyes, and when he was called to leave the work of witness to which he had devoted his long life, summoned all his powers, memory, thought, experience, imagination, faith and prayer, and endeavoured to give as nearly as he might the portrait of Him, whom his hands had touched and his eyes seen, full of grace and truth, a full-orbed star in the tender twilight of the past.

And in the execution of the task he poured out from the Master's lips those precious truths which had become his own not only by the hearing of the ear, but also by the experience of the heart; presented the very core and centre of the teaching; and gave to all of it that lofty and heavenly grace, combined with that homely directness and simplicity, which has made the fourth Gospel at once the most human and the most divine of the four, and has fitted it to be, more than any other composition, the chosen means by which the soul in all ages comes to Christ.

THE NATURE OF THE FATHER

JOHN vi. 57.

IT was a truth which could be spoken to all the world that no man knoweth the Father save the Son and he to whom the Son wills to reveal Him, but the actual unveiling of the Father's face could only be made—that is to say, Jesus could only *will to reveal Him*—to such as are inwardly prepared for so high and honourable a revelation. The mode and result of this personal introduction to the Father, and the kind of intimacy which may therefore exist between the creature and the Creator, are set out, for those who have eyes to see, in the fourth Gospel.

We may describe the contribution which it, in this matter, makes to the teaching of Jesus by a simple human illustration:—There is a vast difference between the knowledge which the outside public and the inner circle may have of an eminent man; between, let us say, the Sir Thomas More, who shone at the court of Henry VIII., and perished on the scaffold, and the father known to Margaret Roper; or between the Cromwell who struck terror into Europe, and the father whose heart broke over the death of Mrs. Claypole, the beloved daughter; or between Lord William Russell as he appeared in the eyes of England, and as he appeared to the intimate love of the wife who spoke of him as her "best and blessed friend." To the public eye the man may be just and benevolent, but distant and enigmatical, admired more than loved, believed in rather than trusted. But in his house he is unveiled; his children know him as the sympathetic friend, the gay and humorous companion; the wife thinks of him as the tender and chivalrous lover. The cold reserves of admiration melt in the warm tides of love. Belief in him seems a chill expression of a platitude; the sentiment is rather a personal, unreserved and passionate trust. He is, of course, the same person; there is a perfect harmony between the two aspects; he could not, perhaps, be what he is without, if he were not what he is within; but they who know him from within would say with some truth that the world which knows him only from without can hardly be said to know him at all.

The Synoptics present Jesus speaking about His Father in that more external way in which the world may know Him; St. John presents Jesus actually showing the Father to receptive hearts. All that the fourth Gospel contains about the Father is an expansion from within of that central Synoptic saying, Matt. xi. 27. But what an expansion it is! Jesus is making a revelation to His own, such as He cannot make to the world. One is carried from the outer into the inner shrine, from the open and bustling judgment of court and senate-house and street, into the intimacy of the house. Here is God the Father shown in such a way that human beings can approach Him, can dare the awful familiarity of contact, and make the blissful experiment of acquaintance.

But the objection may occur: surely, now that this Gospel is put into the world's hands, this introduction to the intimacy of the Father is furnished indiscriminately to all. Certainly those who have made trial of this Way are puzzled to know why every one does not use it to come to the Father. But this objection in a very singular manner answers itself. The secret is not so open as it looks. John Stuart Mill, who found much to admire in the earlier Gospels, pronounced this tedious and incomprehensible; and the more vulgar sort of infidelity delights to hold up these mystical sayings to scorn. The fact is, a certain fitness is presupposed before any one perceives what is in these limpid words. They that love the light come to the light. As the parabolic form of teaching was avowedly designed to ward off the carnal and the curious, so did these words of apparent simplicity establish a test and erect a barrier of their own. It was a primal doctrine of Jesus that pearls should not be cast before swine; it is not the intention of God that men who prefer the husks of error for food should have the pearls of truth to trample on. And it is a very notable fact which is brought to light by the operation of this Gospel in the world, that they who love husks will scorn the pearls and pass by. Here is drawn the picture of God as a Father, so attractive, so convincing, and so accessible, that one would say no man can resist the appeal. But blinded eyes do not see; they even prefer the broken light of the Synoptics to this unclouded glory.

It might seem almost impossible to surpass the picture of fatherly love presented in the parable of the prodigal son. There surely, if anywhere, is *the living Father*.[1] But it has the defects of all images; it limits while defining. Using the noblest human relation to illustrate the divine, it yet circumscribes the divine in some sort to the human. Ungracious as it is to criticise the matchless story, we are bound to observe where it is inadequate, if we are to see how St. John has met the defects. In the parable the Father remains at home awaiting the son's return; there is no room for the idea that the Father should be in any sense present in the far country. Consequently it is the thought of an absent rather than the impulse of a present Father that suggests the return, and the repentance has the air of being the son's spontaneous act rather than the prompting of divine grace. This is, of course, only to say that while God is described in imagery, something must be sacrificed. There will be the implication that He is in one place and not in another, and that His actions are in time, as human actions are.

But in the intimate teaching of Jesus, when He

[1] John vi. 57.

can speak to understanding hearts, He discards parables; and all these limitations disappear. Retaining in the very term "Father" all the suggestions of a patient love and an untiring readiness to forgive, He yet describes God as Spirit—*i.e.*, as "Being emancipated from time and space." Like the wind blowing mysteriously where it lists, He is moving invisible to fulfil His holy purposes everywhere. It is inappropriate to say that He is here or there, or even to say that He is everywhere. For the form of thought by which we are bound to posit all existence in space does not apply to Him. Spirit has no spatial relations. The comparison with an earthly father, or king, or householder, is always limited by the fact that the term of comparison is earthly. Flesh and blood confines the thought to space. But when the term of comparison chosen is the all-pervading, essential, irresistible atmosphere—that is the suggestion of the word Spirit ($\pi\nu\varepsilon\tilde{\upsilon}\mu\alpha$)—we are taken at once into a more expansive region. It is a slight matter for the atmosphere at one and the same time to enwrap the globe, and to minister breath and life to every creature, unembarrassed by the number or variety of kinds. Though the withdrawal of the atmosphere, in an exhausted bell, would immediately terminate the life of any, all are preserved alive by the elastic, accessible, and yet impalpable air. There is the true idea of God. He is not at any time removed from the creature He has made, which only in Him has its being. He is immanent, actively at work; and by an infinity of intelligence and power, which it is not possible for us to conceive, and equally impossible to deny, He can attend to His multiplicity of concerns at one and the same time, with that concentration of energy which a man gives to the least of his small affairs.

Jesus mentions the idea expressly only to show the futility of sacred buildings.[1] But that passage goes farther than at first sight appears. For it immediately suggests the conclusion that the only essential temple of worship is the human spirit, and that of course implies not only an omnipresence of God in a pantheistic sense, but particularly a personal inward relation with every human spirit, a condition which can only be adequately shaped to our imagination by each one regarding himself as the only conscious being in the world, except God, with whom he is at close quarters.

But the thought may be seen to underlie all the teaching of Jesus in this Gospel. As the wind blows, so the Spirit—ever-present, unobserved by human eye—approaches to recreate every human soul.[2] As distinct from the creation, and even the derived life of men, *the Father hath life in Himself*, and it was a peculiar gift transmitted to the Son.[3] This is an important explanation of the term, *the living Father*. There is no delusion commoner than to suppose that life is an ultimate fact, and that every living thing has life in itself. No, says Jesus, God alone is the ultimate fact, and He alone has life in Himself. The creation lives in Him, and at

[1] John iv. 24.   [2] John iii. 8.   [3] John v. 26.

the withdrawal of His life becomes at once inorganic, a charred cinder, a waste of meaningless atoms. Accordingly Jesus is particular to declare that the Father is not a power withdrawn, leaving the universe He has set in motion to proceed mechanically by its own impulse, but *my Father worketh hitherto.*[1] He is in the world always at work, always operating on the minds of men, for *every one that hath heard from the Father and hath learned cometh unto me.*[2] Nothing gives us a clearer idea of the sense that Jesus had of the Father's all-pervasive spirit than this conviction that though He had come into the world to show men the Father, it was always the Father that brought men to Him.

Or, to glance at the teaching of Jesus which appears in the Epistle,—for it is impossible to separate the Epistle and the Gospel; though the one is avowedly a historical record and the other is an effusion of the writer, there is as much of the direct teaching of Jesus in the Epistle as in the Gospel, it is a beautiful saying of the Epistle that God is Light. Like the all-pervasive light, the light which searches all crannies, and attempts all shuttered windows, the light which will not be excluded except by darkness, the heavenly Father is a diffusive, penetrating presence. He assails all souls; He enters chambers of souls even where the greater part of the being is barred against His entrance. He is found lying like a sunbeam on some forlorn and miasmal place, sterilising the

---

[1] John v. 17. [2] John vi. 45.

germs of evil, cheering desolation itself. There may be some souls that are blinded so that they cannot see the light, incapable of God, as a mole of sunshine. But Jesus knows nothing of such. They who do not see the light are, to Him, souls that love darkness rather than the light, men plunged into the obscure caves of selfishness, of worldliness, of sin. He makes no question but that, if they had never so faint a desire for the light, and would open their door to the width of a chink, God, the circumambient light delicately soliciting entrance, would come in.

Jesus explains His own presence in the world as an incarnate beam of that divine Light, which has penetrated into the darkened chambers of human sin, to transform the darkness into light. Again and again He seeks to bring home to men that their rejection of Him is an indication to them of their own blinded state. If they are irritated with Him, the beam of heavenly light shining in the bewildering gloom of the world, that should remind them that they are shutting their souls up against God, the Light. This is so self-evident to Him that He pleads with them, surprised and grieved, to come into His light. *I am come a light into the world, that whosoever believeth on me may not abide in darkness.*[1] As light might dispute with darkness He appeals to men: *I say these things that ye may be saved. Ye will not come to me that ye may have life. How can ye believe that receive glory one of another, and the glory that cometh from the only God ye seek*

[1] John xii. 46.

not?[1] They seem to Him as men who have shut themselves in subterranean cellars to prefer smoking rushlights, and will not come out into the sun, that wooes and waits for them. And yet, as to Him, God, the Light, is the reality, and the darkness is but an obstruction which must disappear, He has an exultant assurance that the uplifted Light will scatter the murk. *I, if I be lifted up, will draw all men unto me.*[2] He never doubts that a time will come when the night shall have passed for ever, and an astonished world, emergent from the gloom, will recognise that Light is triumphant and that He Himself was a beam from that primal Light.

But this image brings us to a truth, which is no longer even an image of so unrestricted and unlimited a character as air and light. There is a thought of God, not obscurely hinted at in all the Gospels, but only expressed as an integral part of the teaching of Jesus by the beloved disciple. The last word could not be spoken until this was said: GOD IS LOVE. Whether Jesus actually uttered those magical words, or only exhibited them in His own person, so that the rapt observer found them instinctively coming to his lips, is a matter of no great importance. The words occur only in the Epistle. The thought throbs all through the Gospel. It is expressed in words which no familiarity can rob of their freshness, words uttered by Jesus Himself perhaps, but in any case learnt only from Him, in that passage where the Light and the Love

---

[1] John v. 34, 40, 44. [2] John xii. 32.

blend into one, where the love of the world is regarded as the light of the world, and men's indifference to the love is explained by their hatred of the Light.[1]

The world, that disordered arena of human freedom and sin, is described as *hating*.[2] It hates God. It hates Jesus. It hates the disciples of Jesus even on account of their faint resemblance to Him. There is no exaggeration in this description. Even in this Christian and civilised community it is no unfrequent experience to run upon this elemental malignity of human nature; you may see that unhallowed fire in the eye, and hear that hiss of the angry tongue which is like the poisonous sting of a serpent. Here in England you may find men who hate God, who force language to express their contempt of Jesus, and overwhelm His witnesses with scurrilous and obscene scorn. Beyond the pale of Christian influence this is far worse. The Moslem's pitiless, bloodthirsty, lustful hatred of the Christian; the fierce and murderous passions which always lurk even under the smile of the yellow races; the internecine savagery and devilry of the races that inhabited the lovely islands of the Pacific, and of vast populations in the dark continent of Africa—certainly justify the broad statement of Jesus by an accumulation of corroborative facts: *The world hates.*

But this world of malignant hate God loves. His love is an eager and active purpose to save.[3] Jesus says: *Thou lovedst me before the foundation of the*

[1] John iii. 16-21.   [2] John xvii. 14.   [3] John iii. 16.

world,[1] before the dark possibilities of the perverted will had come into the region of experience. And yet He could add, *Therefore doth the Father love me because I lay down my life*[2] for the world. God is love in so marvellous a sense that while He loved His obedient and loving Son, He could love also His disobedient and hating world with a redemptive passion, could send His beloved on the errand of salvation, and make it an additional ground of love to His Son, that He was ready to be sacrificed for this graceless world.

This is that truth, GOD IS LOVE; this is the illustration, and the proof of it.

But here, in the very statement of the truth, emerges the old sore problem. If God is Spirit and Light and Love, and God is creator of us all, how comes it that there is a world which hates, a circle of being however trivial and infinitesimal, which is in so blinded and desolate an antagonism to Him that the beloved Son must come and die in order to reconcile it to Him? The difficulty was present to the mind of Jesus, and His solution of it is the only one we possess, and it goes as far as human thought can follow. The world lies in darkness, though God who made it is Love, because it is in the evil one; a usurping and rebellious spirit has acquired power in the diseased will of men; the works of this enemy are in the world on every hand; the Son of Man was manifested to destroy his works. Alone, let us hope, in the wide spaces of the air, and among the uncounted myriads of habitable globes, this globe

---

[1] John xvii. 24.   [2] John x. 17.

has been the scene of this rebellious spirit's enterprises. Every one that commits sin becomes the bond slave of sin, and by a sorrowful inverted new birth the child of this arch-foe of goodness.[1]

But if we ask how God, being Love, could ever allow this rule of the enemy in the world which He made, Jesus gives no direct answer: it does not appear that the question ever presented itself to men in His day: but He leads us to a point of view from which, with a larger outlook, we see a possible explanation, and can with confidence remit the answer to the future. On a certain occasion the disciples asked whether a blind man was born blind as a punishment of his own sins in a previous state, or of his parents' sins before his birth. Jesus made the significant answer: *Neither did this man sin nor his parents; but that the works of God should be made manifest in him.*[2] It would appear that the healing of the blind occasions a rapture of joy which they who have always seen cannot understand; and certainly it exalts the glory of God in a way that would not have been possible if all men had always enjoyed the unbroken exercise of sight. Is there here a clue? The triumph of the Prodigal's return may occasion an ecstasy not otherwise to be obtained; the victory over powers of evil may be a good greater than untempted innocence; a Father manifested in a love which, discouraged by no excess of rebellion, would press to the restoration of the loss through every conceivable sacrifice and pain, might be a Father loved and eternally served as He

[1] John viii. 44. [2] John ix. 3.

could not be even by the hosts of the elder and unfallen sons. Jesus has high thoughts of what He calls *the glory of the Father*, the gleam and splendour of the eternal Light, the divine self-realisation, issuing in a self-revelation. Out of that glory Jesus Himself issued. He showed it, as He shared it. He increased it as He showed it. He certainly saw large illustration, as well as increase of it, in His return to its central magnificence bringing His ransomed with Him.[1]

It was probably therefore to Him self-evident that, while the orders of sinless beings around the throne could glorify the Father, there was a possibility of expansion through conflict, of light emerging brighter out of darkness. A lost world redeemed, a fallen race restored, a company of spirits, cleansed by sacrifice and purged by pain, coming out of great tribulation with palms of victory and songs of joy, might be an accession to that unapproachable glory, the final cause for which the whole creation has come into existence, and is guided through its development. And if this is the luminous thought of Jesus, which of us is in a position to dispute it, or to suggest an explanation more fruitful or more probable?

This then is the supreme revelation of the Father: He is Spirit: He is Light: He is Love. The secular problems, the mystery of sin, the shadow of darkness, the curse of hate, are no disproof of His stainless being, for they all await the manifestation of His being in order to be solved, and banished and destroyed.

[1] John xvii. 22.

It may be said that even this fullest revelation of the Father leaves much that is unexplained, something even that is inexplicable. Perhaps so. But no one can dwell for long together in the atmosphere of these Johannine writings, listening to this heart of the teaching of Jesus, without the discovery of a golden light penetrating the mists, and of a subtle comfort entering the soul. An experience is instituted which is itself the solution of many difficulties.

One begins to engage in the serious conflict of flesh with spirit, of light with darkness, of love with hate. And victories are gained. Is there any bliss like that inclination of the scale when the battle is turned, and the flesh, and the darkness, and the hate are vanquished? That flicker of spiritual flame over the conquered senses; that glimmer of cold dawn over the hurtling shadows of the night; that tremble of melting love in which the floes of hate dissolve and vanish: these are points of bliss which at least to our experience can be in no other way approached. Even with us, is it not possible to draw some inference from the passionate joy of saving a soul, of welcoming a prodigal, of restoring the fallen, of marking the gradual predominance of the better elements in a struggling life? It is surely not inconceivable that it was the largest design of divine love, the mode of producing the most effectual fruits of spiritual gain, and of eternal joy, to admit Satan among the sons of God, that he might go out to the tempting and trial of man. As there could be no question of this subtle Prince of the air ultimately surviving, might he not serve a purpose, and furnish the occasion by which the spiritual thews and manhood of a race might be established? Shall not the Eternal Father be justified in His design of leading the little remnant against the hosts of darkness, of ordaining conflict as the means of victory, and sin as the pre-condition of salvation?

There shall be many sons made perfect through suffering, brought to glory by the arduous way, who shall lie near to the heart of God, and in their excelling triumph fetch new music out of the triple chords: God is Spirit, the living Father; God is Light, and in Him is no darkness; God is Love, and no words can go beyond.

THE NATURE OF THE SON

JOHN x. 30.

THE revelation of an inward life possesses an unfailing interest. We shall remember how fascinating we found the glimpses which Marie Bashkirtseff gave into her experiences, though she was at the best a somewhat mean and sorry little soul. Some years before, we were all captivated by the beautiful, though profoundly saddening, spectacle of Amiel's *Journal Intime.* It would almost seem that if any one, even the most commonplace of persons, could accurately exhibit the workings and development of his mind, we should find a charm in it, simply because it is a human transcript; though of course the supposition is hardly possible, as a perfectly commonplace mind has no power of self-delineation.

But suppose that some document presents to us a genuine insight into the inner life of Jesus; Jesus, who, to say the least of it, is the most wonderful human being that ever lived; Jesus, compared with whose influence on the human race, an ever-increasing influence from the beginning, that of the greatest religious founders, rulers, conquerors, thinkers and authors, seems superficial and evanescent! Suppose it should show us in some degree how He appeared to Himself, what passed in the secret consciousness of the marvellous soul! Suppose we should have, though not written by Himself, something which corresponds to a *Journal Intime* of Jesus!

Now, in a sense, this is what is given us in the Gospel of St. John.

The one thought which always filled the mind of Jesus was that of His Father in heaven. How precisely He was related, and felt Himself to be related, to that invisible Father, the Synoptic Gospels left in obscurity. They made it clear, as we said, that the relation was unique, but that was all.

This Gospel, on the other hand, is very largely occupied with those passages of His teaching which lead an attentive and sympathetic hearer to that mystic meeting-place where the channels of the human soul and the divine being merge into one. The interest of this individuality is unparalleled. We may safely challenge any religion, or any literature, to show anything that corresponds to it. For a careful investigation reveals a consciousness which is at once unmistakably human and unmistakably divine. Nothing could be more undivided, more harmonious, one might almost say more natural, than the soul of Jesus. It betrays none of those incongruous combinations which a scrupulous theology, tenacious of orthodoxy, has discerned in it. There is a person, one person, just as you or I can only be described as one; there is no intermixture of *natures*. But in examining the human soul and becoming convinced of its humanity, we are led to the equal conviction that it is divine. There is a smooth, unbroken continuity in it. One passes, without seam or juncture, from man to God in it, from earth to heaven. Nor, brief as the document is, could the impression be made more distinct or overwhelming by any expansion or elaboration.

The study of this matter in the fourth Gospel can be best disposed in two distinct parts. *First*, there are the references which repeat and confirm those revelations of the person of Jesus which we have detected in the teaching of the Synoptics. *Second*, there are those facts of His consciousness which occur in the earlier Gospels only in faint hints and far-off echoes, or not at all, but in St. John are made quite distinct, and if not disconnected from those more public utterances, yet, as the intimate expression of a great soul showing Himself to His friends, become virtually a new revelation.

This first line of study may be followed out in the present section; and it need hardly be said that the value of it lies in the discovery that the two sources, so different in form as St. John and the Synoptics, absolutely agree in the main outlines of the personality of Jesus; an agreement, be it observed, which is very intelligible so long as we regard all the four Gospels as the product of the immediate circle which surrounded Jesus, and saw and heard Him during His earthly career; but an agreement which becomes remarkable, and rich in evidential value, if further inquiry requires us to bring the fourth Gospel down into the middle of the second century. For, while it is easily conceivable that a second-century writer would servilely copy the documents of an earlier day; it is a very curious problem how such a writer, with a complete change of style and form and terminology, could yet so accurately portray the identical unique consciousness which the artless contemporary records had presented.

The second line of study must be deferred to another section. It leads us to that fact of the consciousness of Jesus, which might be inferred from many hints in the Synoptics, but is certainly never expressly mentioned in them—viz., His preexistence.

Now to follow out those features of personality which we have already traced in the earlier study, as they appear in St. John. Jesus described Himself, we saw, as Messiah, under the adapted designation of Son of Man, and He also not obscurely indicated His claim to be called the Son of God.

1. First, to examine the suggestion of His Messiahship:—Notwithstanding the complete difference of form, we find that His teaching in this Gospel not only is the same in fact, but also follows the same singularly marked intonation, as it did in the Synoptics. Here, as there, He is from the time of the Baptism aware that He is Messiah, and yet here, as there, in all conversations with Jews, who cherished the most misleading associations in connection with the title, He sedulously avoids using the word itself. It is just the same situation that we examined before; He is bound to make a claim;

He is bound to identify Himself with one who was expected; but He is bent on disconnecting Himself from the expectations which had been forming in the popular mind.

Thus, though in this Gospel it would seem that from the first the disciples were of opinion that they had found in Him the Messiah,[1] He did not claim the title Himself, except outside the borders of Judaism in a conversation with a Samaritan, where no misleading worldly hopes would prejudice the value of the disclosure.[2] His reserve on this subject is even more marked in St. John than elsewhere. For here even the form of Peter's ultimate confession, which has been dictated to him by the Father, is not, Thou art the Messiah, as in the Synoptics, but Thou art the Holy One of God.[3] Even when Martha, towards the end of the life, says to Him; "I have believed that Thou art the Messiah,"[4] He makes no reply. And especially, when the prejudiced Jews pressed Him with the request, "If thou art the Christ, tell us plainly"[5] He refused to tell them plainly. He simply pointed to His works, to His character, to His word, those inward and spiritual witnesses which were to regenerate the idea of the Messiah before He could accept the name; and proceeded to declare that His questioners were devoid of that moral fitness which could alone

---

[1] John i. 45.
[2] John iv. 25 : The woman evidently expected Messiah simply to be the declarer of truth, not a national liberator and the founder of a political throne.
John vi. 69.   [4] John xi. 27.   [5] John x. 24.

recognise His office as He demanded that it should be recognised.

All this not only echoes what we found in the Synoptics, but it echoes the precise tone of the language which Jesus employed on the subject.

Yet here, as there, He is explicit in claiming the prophetic office, as when He quotes in reference to Himself the adage *A prophet hath no honour in his own country*.[1] And possibly He classes Himself with the prophets generally and with John the last of the order particularly, when He says, using the plural number, *We speak that we do know, and bear witness of that we have seen*.[2] Then in these discourses He delights to refer to Himself as "The Sent": *Whom He sent him ye believe not; this is the work of God, that ye believe on him whom He hath sent: I am from Him, and He sent me: whom the Father sanctified and sent into the world: whom Thou didst send, even Jesus Christ*.[3] This was, of course, a claim, without using the name Messiah, to be that messenger described frequently by the prophets of the Old Testament, who was to come from God, the messenger whom the Rabbis called Messiah.

Here, too, though not so frequently, occurs His chosen appellation The Son of Man. Some dozen times it occurs. As in the vision of Daniel from which we saw reason to think He took the name, He was to be the Judge of the world because He was the Son of Man.[4] And the precise relation of this

[1] John iv. 44.   [2] John iii. 11.
[3] John v. 38, vi. 29, vii. 29, x. 36, xvii. 3.   [4] John v. 27.

term to the more familiar name Messiah, the hesitating or questioning identification of the two in the public mind, we are able to see in the inquiry of the multitude, "We have heard out of the law that the Messiah abideth for ever, and how sayest thou the Son of Man must be lifted up? Who is this Son of Man?"[1] Here it is made plain, plainer even than in the Synoptics, that He used the title Son of Man as a veiled declaration of His Messiahship, and that His hearers were actually impelled by His use of it to make the kind of search which He intended to provoke.

And here, naturally, even more than in the external record of His words and of the effect they produced, it is plain that His mode of self-designation became intelligible to *His own*. Slowly but surely He conveyed to them the conviction of His consciousness, that He was not only that prophet of whom Moses wrote, and that heavenly messenger described in the Book of Isaiah and seen in the vision of Daniel, coming in the clouds of heaven, but also One whom even prophets desired to see but could not fully forecast, because He was more than the ancient religion dreamed, a Being whom nothing but the fact of His manifestation could adequately declare. The course of St. John's Gospel exhibits the growing impression of this revelation, as, in language to which there is nothing parallel in the first gospels,[2] He explained, *I am the light of the world, he that followeth me shall not walk in darkness;* or, *I am the way, the truth and the life; no man cometh to*

[1] John xii. 34. [2] John viii. 12.

the Father but through me;[1] *or, I am the resurrection and the life, he that believeth on me though he was dead yet shall he live;*[2] *or, he that hath seen me hath seen the Father;*[3] *or, he that honoureth not the son honoureth not the Father who hath sent him.*[4]

II. But these expressions, already too remarkable to be appropriate in merely human lips, prepare the way for that discovery made in these more intimate discourses which gives to the fourth Gospel a character of its own.

The title *Son of God* was certainly claimed, if not in so many words, when Jesus said, *No man knoweth the Father save the Son*,[5] in that significant and central passage to which we have had so frequent occasion to refer in the earlier sections. It was suggested also, as we saw, in some of the Synoptic parables. But it never became a familiar expression of His inner consciousness, still less an acknowledged term applied to Him by outsiders. In the discourses of the fourth Gospel, however, we find Jesus freely and explicitly claiming it. After that point marked in the Synoptics,[6] at which Peter distinctly addressed Him as the Son of the living God, the appellation was, we gather from St. John, frankly accepted by Jesus and employed by the disciples and other members of His circle. And as it became the most familiar and the most appropriate designation of Him, St. John loses all count of the fact that there had been a time in the ministry when it was used with reserve, a time even before the disciples them-

---
[1] John xiv. 6.   [2] John xi. 25.   [3] John xiv. 9.
[4] John v. 23.   [5] Matt. xi. 27.   [6] Matt. xvi. 16.

selves had recognised it, and he introduces the expression into the earliest discourses that he records. Whatever steps there might be in the discovery of His heart that He was the Son of God, the discovery, once made to men, would naturally override every other thought, and gradually supersede every other title.

We must now therefore examine the revelations of His consciousness on this important point. And on the threshold of the subject comes that significant mode of speech, according to which He refrained from coupling Himself and His disciples together in a common sonship to God. If He encouraged them to speak of Our Father, He did not include Himself with them in such an address. Where He wished to speak of the Father who was common to them and Him He adopted the particular expression, *My Father and your Father.* And thus, though the actual occasion of the phrase throws it into the lips of His adversaries, it was, we may rest assured, a phrase of His own: "He said that God was *his own* (ἴδιον) Father"—His Father, that is, in a peculiar and appropriate sense—"making Himself equal with God."[1] If there was some malicious exaggeration of His enemies in this latter charge, as Jesus seems to imply in the answer He makes, *the Son can do nothing of Himself*, at least there is none in the former phrase which exactly conveys the thought running through all these discourses, that God is His own Father. In another case He defines still more nicely the precise position which He was

[1] John v. 18.

conscious of holding. " Thou, being a man, makest thyself God," said His enemies. To which He replied with the most forbearing expostulation, *Say ye of Him, whom the Father sanctified and sent into the world, Thou blasphemest; because I said, I am the Son of God?*[1] Here He just as certainly claims this peculiar title, as He implicitly rebuts the precise form of the allegation made against Him.

And indeed, if not a word of His own coining, none expresses the thought which His consciousness is everywhere suggesting better than Only-begotten.[2] We only hesitate to claim it as a self-chosen appellative because of the uncertainty to which allusion has already been made, whether iii. 16-21 is to be understood as the discourse of Jesus, or the comment of the evangelist.

Jesus is conscious that the Father has given to Him, as the Son in this unique sense, the divine prerogative of judgment,[3] as we found stated and depicted with suitable colours, in the Synoptics, and that other divine prerogative of having life in Himself.[4] He is conscious even that the Father reveals to Him all that *He* does, as if no secrets were kept from the Son in His bosom.[5]

Nothing could possibly surpass this sense of an intimacy in which two persons are literally merged in one.

In the Synoptics we saw how much was implied

---

[1] John x. 36: Dr. Dale has pointed out in his *Christian Doctrine* the remarkable fact that Jesus never prays *with* His disciples, but only *for* them. He does not use the *Our Father* which He prescribes to them. [2] John iii. 16, 17.
[3] John v. 22. [4] John v. 26. [5] John v. 20.

in the sinlessness of Jesus. And here again the precise point of the union between the Father and the Son seems to lie in the unimpeded relation of a sinless being. The will of the Son has never deviated a hair's breadth from that of the Father. This introduces an exquisite ethical meaning into a relationship which might otherwise seem to be merely ontological. As contrasted with the slave of sin, He is the Son that abideth in the Father's house for ever.[1] This ethical tie is brought out in a previous expression: *He that sent me is with me; He hath not left me alone; for I do always the things that are pleasing to Him.*[2] He finds an evident delight in dwelling upon this identity of His own will with the will of God, which is a good definition of sinlessness. It occurs again and again: *I seek not my own will but the will of Him that sent me;*[3] *I am come down from heaven, not to do my own will but the will of Him that sent me.*[4] It is, He says, because He seeks the glory of Him that sent Him, that He is true and no unrighteousness is in Him.[5]

This consciousness that He is without sin is the most remarkable thing in the records of human nature. He is constrained to utter it from a sense of truth. If He shrank from it, it would involve Him in an untruth which would itself be sin. *I keep His word,*[6] He says. This is a source of unspeakable rest and joy to Him: *I have kept my Father's commandments and abide in His love.*[7] Or

---

[1] John viii. 35, 36.   [2] John viii. 29.   [3] John v. 30.
[4] John vi. 38.   [5] John vii. 18.   [6] John viii. 55.
[7] John xv. 10.

perhaps never did He give a more revealing flash of that serene, untroubled union which He always maintained with His Father, than when He answered the agitation of His disciples about the earthly food by the saying: *My meat is to do the will of Him that sent me.*[1] Thus He mounts to that daring question, which, in the light of this investigation, we cannot take in any limited or partial sense, *Which of you convinces me of sin?*[2] Nay, the very principle of sin itself, the ruler of this world, comes, and *finds nothing in Him.*[3] He has, so His exulting heart assures Him, *overcome the world.*[4]

This consciousness of a relation with the Father, entirely undisturbed by sin, is so remarkable—and how remarkable it is one only realises by trying to conceive any other person who ever lived employing similar language—that a certain school of modern scholars has sought to rest the whole argument for the divinity of Jesus on this, and this alone. Following this line of thought, Wendt would suggest that He was the Son of God, because He was sinless, as if by such a moral victory, by such a course of harmonious, sinless development, He reached for the first time this unequalled relation with the Father. Let us fully recognise that such a way of regarding the matter is more fruitful, and in the end more conservative of the historical authenticity of the Christian gospel, than the perfectly abstract dogma, that He was sinless because He was God. This conclusion of a high and dry orthodoxy is utterly

---

[1] John iv. 34.
[2] John viii. 46.
[3] John xiv. 30.
[4] John xvi. 33.

sterile; it robs His temptation of all reality, for how can God be tempted?—and it puts an impassable gulf between us and Him. In this as in other matters Wendt and the followers of Ritschl have raised a too vehement protest against a theological position which, as irrational, ceased to be religious.

But if we are determined to follow scrupulously the guidance of His own teaching, and of that insight which He Himself affords into His own consciousness, we must here part company from Wendt as decidedly as from His opponents; for the wonderful prayer, John xvii. is unequivocal in showing that the Sonship was not achieved, but essential and eternal. His plea that, being sanctified and sent into the world by the Father, He might without blasphemy say *I am the Son of God*,[1] is decisive of the question that the Sonship antedated His mission. To this we are bound to hold, and yet, if we are not to deprive the events of this story of all spiritual value we are bound also to admit that, conscious of this essential and unbroken Sonship as He became in the course of His life, He yet was born into this world truly and absolutely man. Reflect on the narrative even of this fourth Gospel, and you perceive that He was man in such a sense, that His remaining sinless must be regarded as the heroism of a moral energy, and as truly miraculous as it would be if *we* had remained sinless through life.

III. There is one other point which has to be ob-

[1] John x. 33-38.

served to complete the survey of those elements in the teaching of the fourth Gospel which expound and confirm what was said in the Synoptics on the nature of Jesus.

If in this gospel the majestic claims involved in the consciousness of Jesus are brought into clear relief, here also the humble and prayerful dependence of the Son on the Father is expressed in almost every discourse, however fragmentary. Indeed, the humanity, in the sense of subjection to, and reliance on, the invisible God, is emphasised more than in the Synoptics, where it is taken for granted. It almost seems as if in some of the sayings there is a conscious purpose to combat or forestall the heresy that would deny the proper manhood of Jesus. Thus He describes Himself as *a man who has told you the truth*.[1] It produces a decided impression to enumerate the repeated repudiations of ever acting apart from His Father. In every variety of detail He affirms that He only does what He sees the Father do, only says what He hears from the Father, only gives what the Father has given to Him. *My teaching is not mine, but His that sent me:*[2] *I do nothing of myself, but as the Father taught me I speak these things:*[3] *I am come in my Father's name:*[4] *as I hear I judge.*[5] One of the most striking differences between Him and an ordinary man is that we, as a

---

[1] John viii. 40 : He uses the word ἄνθρωπον in a peculiar way, not merely an indefinite, unemphatic "one" which would be expressed by the article, or at most by a pronoun, but as the specific designation of humanity in contrast with Deity.

[2] John vii. 16.   [3] John viii. 28.
[4] John v. 43.   [5] John v. 30.

rule, are so much more independent. We utter our own ideas, do what we think right, act on our own responsibility: He is entirely engaged in copying, repeating, acting for, Another.

Thus this life is one of continuous prayer. His language seems always trembling on the edge of prayer: *Father, I thank Thee that Thou heardest me, and I knew that Thou hearest me always.*[1] When He would send a great boon on men, He says, *I will pray the Father.*[2] Such a picture of careful and prayerful dependence on God was never before seen. As He felt, it rendered the two indistinguishable: *I am in the Father: the Father is in me:*[3] *all mine are Thine and Thine mine.*[4]

This modest merging of Himself in God, which identifies the Son of Man and the Son of God with the Father, has sometimes been cited to show that He is only a man like ourselves. Surely the fact proves just the opposite. This human soul which does not breathe or move except as the instrument of the Father's will, is, by that very fact, God manifested in the sphere of human life. He is from heaven. To hear and to see Him is to hear and see God. To reject Him is to reject the Father. He is the divine Being brought into contact with human souls, made a bread for the human spirit to eat and live. When the Son of God is manifested to a man, faith in Him becomes reconciliation with the Father, the discovery and worship of God.[5] *Now is the Son of Man glorified and God is glorified in Him.*[6]

[1] John xi. 41.   [2] John xiv. 16.   [3] John xiv. 10.
John xvii. 10.   [5] John ix. 35, 36.   [6] John xiii. 31.

Nothing can lessen the mystery of this great religious phenomenon. But our study of this *Journal Intime* of Jesus lays bare to us a purely, a typically human soul, prepared, developed, kept, growing up in a perfectly human way ; and yet, wonderful to state, quite free from sin, maintaining a life of free, spontaneous, unbroken, identity with God ; with this result that in Him is God's perfect revelation, not only of the human, but also of the divine, indeed of Himself. In the only way that is even conceivable to man, the invisible and eternal spirit, God, has become through an incarnation, manifest to man.

I and the Father are one.

THE PRE-EXISTENCE OF JESUS

JOHN i. 18

WE come now to that part of the Teaching—that part, let us say, of the *Journal Intime* of Jesus—which reveals certain elements of His self-consciousness, never explicitly revealed in the Synoptics. And when we observe closely what these are, and how this part of His inner life was manifested to Himself, we shall feel small wonder that facts of so transcendent and so unusual a texture should have obtained no lodgment in the merely hearsay reports of His teaching. Here was certainly a truth which could only be communicated to sympathetic hearers. If it should be mentioned to the unsympathetic it would be at the best unintelligible, at the worst a rock of offence. It was a truth which, stated baldly in an unpropitious atmosphere, might make no impression at all, or might be attributed to delirations of a heated fancy. If He was to state it in a way to produce conviction, it must decidedly be stated to the initiated, to men so trained and prepared that He could admit them into an unreserved confidence and unbosom Himself to them.

For there is a great deal in even the meanest

human being that can never be unfolded unless it chance that a suitable audience presents itself. Even we are not capable of revealing ourselves to everybody: to some natures we cannot reveal ourselves at all. The secrets of our being lie buried down below the reach of conjecture; they come up into the light only when reverent and understanding eyes are there to see.

Now this seems to have been the fact: when in the course of that natural and normal development, which we have repeatedly seen must be assumed in the case of Jesus as of others, His consciousness reached its full and legitimate unfolding—an unfolding which was not to be expected at the beginning but only as the result of the human life which He came into the world to live—there lay in the very core of His consciousness, like the ovary filled with seed at the centre of a ripened flower, the unequivocal knowledge, or at least let us say, the unfaltering inference, that His existence had not begun, like that of other men, with the human birth, but rather before the foundation of the world in the past eternity of God. This conviction, appearing in the maturity of that unique consciousness, demands a careful study. To careless and superficial observers it would be a matter of incredulity or derision if it were observed at all. But, happily for the delicate bloom of spiritual fact, and the fine sheen of the pearls of God, they remain entirely beyond the range of eyes that are incapable of learning and profiting.

Imagine for a moment a diver who has taken a deep and desperate plunge into the abyss of waters in order to fetch up a treasure from the floor of the sea. The stound of the dive, the rush and the gurgle of the element, the difficulty of the enterprise, perhaps even the absorption in the object which he has in view—may drive from his recollection for the moment all thought of the upper air from which he came. In the same way one may conceive Jesus, the eternal Son of God, who has of set purpose cast aside His prerogatives and the enjoyment of the heavenly world, that He may dive down into the depths of humanity and recover the treasure that is lost. When first we observe Him, He is in the depths. The search and the promise of finding occupy His whole attention. We ourselves can think of nothing but His heroic and self-sacrificing toil. But time passes, and presently, His work achieved or in the way of achievement, He begins to consider a return to the place from which He came. Like the glimmering light through the green waters, which brightens and broadens as the diver nears the surface, the conviction clears in the mind of Jesus, before He emerges into His proper atmosphere, a growing conviction of the glory which He had with the Father before the world was, and of His rapidly approaching restoration to the glory.

If we are to apprehend a fact so mysterious, and so removed from the region of a common experience, we have but one course to adopt. We must dismiss preconceived opinions and adhere very closely to our records. We cannot, at least at the beginning, allow ourselves any speculation. Philosophising is quite out of place. Our one thought is to penetrate

—to put ourselves into the spiritual attitude in which we are capable of penetrating—the consciousness of Jesus. We must be open-eared for His words, and open-hearted to their meaning. On the suspicion of an improper spirit He will withdraw, veil Himself, become impenetrable.

There are, as has been hinted, two lines within which our discussion moves, and though it gives to the inquiry an air of dogmatism, in the interests of clearness we are perhaps justified in laying these lines down beforehand :

1. The fact of His pre-existence does not come to light except as the outcome of His fully developed consciousness, and it is not therefore expressed until a late stage in His teaching.

2. As such, and in its natural place, it occurs with perfect distinctness.

I. We must realise the importance of giving a due recognition to this first fact, a fact which has been seldom or never recognised in systematic theology, or in popular preaching. And because the fact has not been observed, it has been easy to bring the silence of the first three Gospels as a powerful argument against the pre-existence of Jesus. In those sources there is frequent reference made to what will follow on the termination of His earthly career. He will pass into the heavens ; He will sit at the right hand of God : He will come again to judge the world. But no reference is made to the fact that He occupied that exalted condition before He came. Just to take one instance out of many—when the Sadducees question the reality of the resurrection, Jesus does not, as in the case of Nicodemus, appeal to what He has seen in the invisible world, but relies upon an argument from the letter of the Law. If it be said that there is one place, in the Parable of the Vineyard, where the words of God, " I will send my Son," might imply that He was existing in heaven before He was sent, we find ourselves precluded from this argument by the fact that the same language is used about the servants, the prophets, whose pre-existence in heaven it is not proposed to maintain.[1]

Of course when we read Matthew, Mark and Luke, we naturally carry into them truths which we have derived from other writers; so that it startles us to find that if our New Testament consisted *only* of these three documents we should have no reason to say that Jesus existed before the miraculous birth of Bethlehem. Yet this is certainly the fact. From this fact it has been argued, that as the oldest sources of the teaching know nothing of pre-existence, its occurrence later cannot be referred to Jesus Himself. Nor is there any way of meeting this difficulty except by recognising that the consciousness of pre-existence was not there in the mind of Jesus as a constant and dominating factor from the beginning of His life, but emerged somewhat in the manner which has been suggested.

This is so important a point that it may be well to emphasise it in another way. The idea of pre-existence was common in antiquity, derived, probably enough, from Indian sources. Pythagoras and Plato both definitely taught that the soul enters into the

[1] Mark xii. 2, 4, 6 (Matt. xxi. 33; Luke xx. 9).

world from a previous state of existence through the waters of Lethe. The idea occurs in the Book of Wisdom, one of the most familiar of books in the time of Jesus. And even in the New Testament itself there is one passage, John ix. 2, which implies it. Nay more, the idea is suggested by some transient facts in every one's consciousness. It is difficult to read Wordsworth's "Ode on the Intimations of Immortality from the Recollections of Childhood," without a haunting sensation that the poet's assertion—

> Not in entire forgetfulness
> And not in utter nakedness;
> But trailing clouds of glory do we come
> From God, who is our home,

is the expression of our own conviction.

Considering then that the opinion is in itself sufficiently natural, and was as a matter of fact widely entertained in antiquity, we should certainly have been prepared to find Jesus saying from the beginning and constantly, that He had come into the world from a previous state of existence. And we might have expected that He would place His difference from the common experience principally in this that He had not passed through Lethe, but was here in the world laden with distinct recollections of the heaven from which He had come. Even with the impressions we gather from other parts of the New Testament, we certainly could not have been surprised to find Him basing the whole body of His exoteric teaching on the fact of His consciousness, and claiming the belief of His hearers because He spoke from a personal experience of that invisible world which men have always dreamed of, but never visited.

When therefore we find the whole body of His teaching as it is contained in our three earliest sources without a trace of this thought, we must admit that an explanation is required, nor can we be astonished that many serious students have been staggered. Wendt absolutely denies the pre-existence of Jesus altogether, and even Beyschlag feels bound to explain away the passages in St. John which bear upon this point.

But while an explanation is certainly required, I venture to believe that it is found in that idea, which has all along proved so fruitful, the idea of the natural development of Jesus. Only by degrees, and in a perfectly normal way, did His consciousness unfold. The exigencies of His humiliation required that in this thing too He should not be separated from His brethren. The truths which completed His teaching were not realised even by Him in the beginning. Facts even in Himself did not emerge until the appointed time. Accordingly this truth, which would break upon Him with a shock of inward surprise, and would be cherished and revolved in secret long before He would think of uttering it, did not occur till the later passages of His teaching. And even then, in all probability, it produced no definite impression on ordinary or unreceptive hearers. Only to one who lay in His bosom could it be unfolded. In the Synoptic tradition it found no place. In the soul of John it found a place. To him it became the explanation of everything, the key-note of all the teaching. Every recollection of those far-distant days was tinged with it, and he could hardly recall a single discourse which did not to his glowing recollection ring with the mighty truth: "The Word became flesh and dwelt among us."

II. But this has brought us to the other limiting line which marks out our discussion. In this fourth Gospel, not only is the fact of the pre-existence assumed by the writer in the opening passage on the Logos, but it occurs on the lips of Jesus Himself, as a part of His teaching concerning Himself, in a way so distinct that no one who had not a theory to maintain would ever dream of denying it.

No man, says Jesus, *hath ascended into heaven, but He that descended out of heaven, even the Son of Man which is in heaven:*[1] *what then if ye should behold the Son of Man ascending where He was before:*[2] *before Abraham was, I am:*[3] *I speak the things which I have seen with the Father:*[4] *now, O Father, glorify Thou me with Thine own self with the glory which I had with Thee before the world was:*[5] *Thou lovedst me before the foundation of the world.*[6]

Nor is it only that these statements are explicit and beyond the reach of misunderstanding. The

---

[1] John iii. 13.
[2] John vi. 62: Wendt would have us believe that this verse is merely an insertion of the redactor, saying that it breaks the course of the argument. But no one ever felt this until the passage was studied with a view of explaining away inconvenient sayings.   [3] John viii. 58.
[4] John viii. 38.   [5] John xvii. 5.   [6] John xvii. 24.

supposition of the conviction in the heart of Jesus may be traced, underlying all the discourses, especially that central discourse about the Bread of Life sent down from heaven, which is contrasted with the teaching of even so great an earthly prophet as Moses himself.[1]

When, therefore, scholars like Wendt and Beyschlag set themselves to explain away these sayings, and to show that the words do not mean what they so precisely and variously express; and when it is argued that Jesus only intended to say that He had pre-existed in idea, and was known to God in the way that Jeremiah said he was known before he was conceived in the womb; we, with common English minds, are baffled by the arbitrariness of German theologians; we are disposed to say, " Prove if you will that John is incorrect, or that these sayings do not come from Jesus at all; but in the name of simple straightforwardness, do not attempt to maintain that these distinct statements are not intended to convey the truth that Jesus existed as a conscious person before He came into the world."

And when these scholars, and Wendt especially, carry their prejudice so far as to say that if these passages did mean what they say, that would discredit the fourth Gospel as a historical source altogether, because of the contradiction thus involved to the teaching in the other three, they are forgetting how they themselves have established on independent grounds the authenticity of St. John, and have more than once insisted on the kind of

[1] John vi. 32, 33.

development in the thought and self-consciousness of Jesus which is required in order to solve the present difficulty. When we have found the strongest reason to place confidence in the contents of this fourth Gospel as a whole, we are bound to posit the teaching in its entirety, and endeavour to understand it, not thinking of so illogical a course as that of abruptly dismissing whatever occurs here and not in the other sources. If an idea like this of pre-existence does not square with our presuppositions we must revise our presuppositions. Certainly we must not discard the idea unless we find it incomprehensible in the light of the book, its genesis and development, as we have come to understand it.

But so far from being inconsistent with that view of the Gospel of St. John which we have been bound to take, this truth and the manner in which it occurs is in perfect harmony with that view. By our hypothesis the evangelist, after brooding for years on the thought of Jesus, and working out His notions in spiritual practice, grasped the flowers and fruit of all He taught, and brought this last result to interpret what went before. And further we have seen all along that the unfolding consciousness of Jesus could not possibly be intelligible to one who was still entangled in the process. It was absolutely necessary to wait and to see whither it would lead. Gradually He gained the knowledge of His mission; gradually came the certainty that He was Messiah; slowly He won the knowledge of His unique Sonship; slowly He apprehended all, the suffering and the death that was involved in His task. How natural, therefore, that the long assimilation of His experience in communion with the Father could alone bring out the fact that He had been with the Father so from the beginning, and had been at the shaping of that Universe in which He was now, by a voluntary surrender, a created part! And if this was the process of His own discovery, how inevitable was it that only a few, and they gradually, would understand it, and that only in such vivid and spiritually logical natures as those of St. John and St. Paul could it attain its first clear expression and formulation!

And one other argument may be added. When we are compelled to recognise in these discourses of St. John that this *was* part of the consciousness of Jesus, just as we were compelled to recognise the sense of perfect sinlessness, can we say, with any show of reason, that the one is more incredible than the other? Both pre-existence and sinlessness are facts of which we have no experience: if anything, we have more immediate witness in our own consciousness of the former than of the latter. Wendt and Beyschlag are most strenuous in maintaining the sinlessness. What reason is there, except in the demands of a foregone conclusion, for denying the pre-existence? Fairly stated, surely the notion of a stainless human being growing up, and by virtue of inward effort *becoming the Son of God*, and attaining thereby to a share of His most exalted prerogatives is encumbered with far more serious difficulties than the notion which is, as we have said, distinctly presented by this Evangelist, and was afterwards worked out a little further in the Pauline writings—viz., that the Son of God, a Being existent in the Being of God before all time, the Being in whose image ideally man was made, was enabled by the eternal and unlimited power of God to enter into the field of human history, and take His place, in no counterfeit sense, among the sons of men. Where we are dealing confessedly with transcendental phenomena, and with a fact which every one admits stands alone in human experience—a fact therefore, in the very nature of the case, not of discovery but of revelation—we may claim that the interpretation presented in the New Testament is, apart from all question of authority, intrinsically the most credible. Nothing is gained by this modern attempt to discredit the pre-existence of Jesus—nothing even in the way of rationality or credibility. The theory which Wendt suggests is open to all the objections of a materialistic and essentially unbelieving criticism; nothing further can be said against the view that Jesus was a true man, by virtue of His having consented to divest Himself of all those elements in His eternal nature which were not merely human, and that consequently in no feigned or docetic experience, but in a manner perfectly normal, He passed through all the gradations and developments of a proper human life, *including the necessary obliteration at first from His consciousness, and the gradual recognition afterwards, of His pre-existence in an eternal state.*

The difficulty indeed, does not, we may believe, lie in the idea itself, but in the silence of the Synoptic evangelists. This silence we have endeavoured to explain, with what success the reader, after prayerful thought, must judge. But as a further makeweight against that perplexing silence let him remember that St. Paul, who chronologically is an earlier witness than even the first of the evangelists, certainly entertained no doubt that Jesus came into the world from a pre-existent state.

But if this fact of the pre-existence, as it is presented in the Johannine teaching of Jesus, may be considered established, observe that it is further corroborated by the immediate explanation it offers of much which occurs not only in the fourth, but in the earlier Gospels. That unapproachable union and identity of Jesus with God, which never seems sufficiently accounted for by the mere fact of sinlessness—a fact which has almost a negative aspect —receives a natural interpretation. A human being, who was also in the centre of His personality, however unconscious He might be of it at first, identical with the supra-sensible and supra-human Son that must be posited by any theory of God which does not leave Him a solitary, isolated, unrelated Being; such a human being, I say, would instinctively, apart from conscious reflection or formulated speech, exhibit the characteristic which is most striking in the portraiture of the Gospels. That air of authority which was observable from the outset of His career,[1] apart from any expressed claim, or words of sounding assumption, receives a legitimate explanation. There is reason for that indefinable

[1] Mark i. 27.

impression which He makes at the very first, that He has arrived with a mission. To fall back on the image which in some ways comes nearest to the situation: He comes through the sea, the surge and the surf of His humiliation, and appears among us, the lost and perishing mariners on the shore of humanity; and He carries in His hand the rope, which is attached to the eternal and immutable being of God.

And it is here, in this crowning summit of His teaching concerning Himself, that we for the first time see exhibited the length and breadth of His saving love.

It was this discovery which, when it was made, prostrated those first disciples, John and Paul, before His feet in grateful adoration. He who had been among them in the meek garb of a humanity like their own, He who had drawn them into an open familiarity and called them friends, He who had made no mention of His majesty, but veiled it rather, permitting it to speak unobtrusively for itself, was out of the bosom of the Father, the radiant Being through whom the world was made! There was love indeed, the very height of selfless, unprotesting love! Were we to lose sight of this supreme factor in His manifestation, we should reduce His love to comparatively commonplace dimensions. Were He only a man, doing his duty, loving others as a man does, dying for the truth, there would be a love attractive and beautiful enough, no doubt, in its way. But for proof of a love which can stir the world like a passion, subdue the scoffer, and humble the proud, a love which touches the quick because it comes from the quick of the infinite heart, it is essential to recognise *who this was* that wore so lowly a mien. So only can we apprehend what sacrifice was involved. Even the sacrifice of the cross is after all only an incident in the sacrifice of one who consented to lay aside His glory, and lose the consciousness of His own appropriate being, in the redemptive passage through the ways of a lost humanity.

ETERNAL LIFE

JOHN iii. 15.

WHERE in the Synoptic teaching Jesus uses the term, the kingdom of God, in the Johannine teaching He substitutes *eternal life*. That the two were synonymous on His lips is suggested even by certain passages in Mark and Luke. For example, in the precisely parallel verses, Mark ix. 45 and 47, it may be observed that where *life* is used in the first, *kingdom of God* is used in the second. *It is good for thee to enter into life halt, rather than having thy two feet to be cast into hell: it is good for thee to enter into the kingdom of God with one eye, rather than having two eyes to be cast into hell.* In Luke xviii. 18 and 24 the identity is still more explicit. "Good Master, what shall I do to inherit *eternal life?*" asks the ruler. Jesus in His answer says, *How hardly shall they that have riches enter into the kingdom of God!*

But the intention of the fourth evangelist to employ the one term in the place of the other is announced very early, in the third chapter. In that passage Jesus interprets His own oracular utterance, *Except a man be born anew he cannot see the kingdom of God*,[1] by the expression, *So must the Son of Man be lifted up, that whosoever believeth may in Him have eternal life*.[2] After that, eternal life occurs frequently, and kingdom of God not at all, in the Gospel.

This is a very important fact to establish, and it is too often overlooked. It would seem that *kingdom of God* was the best term to use in speaking to Jews who were already furnished by their prophets with many theocratic ideas and expectations, which the phrase kindled into life; but it was not a suitable term for the world at large, which drew its conceptions of kingship from Ptolemies, Seleuci, and latterly the idolatrous *dominium* of the Roman Cæsars. If mankind in all ages was to be reached, a simpler, a more universal, a more inward and mystical term must be employed. Kingship was a variable and transitory idea. A time may even come when it will have only an archaic meaning. But life, eternal life, remains always, and always strikes home.

> 'Tis life, whereof our nerves are scant
> More life, and fuller, that we want.

We all chafe at the invidious restraint which death imposes upon us, and are affected with a disdainful indignation at the "smell of mortality."

Accordingly Jesus translated His own phrase out of the language of Judaism into the language of mankind. He used the original term in His ministry among His people, but He intimated that He would use the translation among men at large. He had

---

[1] John iii. 3.   [2] John iii. 15.

come to establish the kingdom of God, the divine sovereignty in the rebellious human will, to gather and train souls from the rival kingdom of sin, and through regenerate men to establish even on earth a dominion of righteousness which would be connected with the everlasting kingdom of the heavens. This meant, in other words, that He had come bringing life to the world, that men *might have life and have it more abundantly*.[1] For the realm of sin is the realm of death. Absolute harmony with the will of God is life, and that alone; for He is the living God, and all live unto Him. If men are dead in a spiritual sense, He is no longer their God; He is not the God of the dead, but of the living.

But when He substituted this more abstract and more personal idea of eternal life for the richly coloured and far-reaching phrase, the kingdom of God, He certainly had no intention of surrendering that earlier image. On the contrary, the two ideas were to be retained, as they are in our four Gospels taken together, to interpret one another. One might almost say that until we have observed that the terms are identical we never quite understand either. Like the terms "Son of Man" and "Son of God," that go to make up the designation of Jesus Himself, the terms "eternal life" and "kingdom of God" go to make up the conception of the boon which He has introduced into the world.

We may anticipate therefore much profit from considering in more detail the identity of the two ideas. And this we can do by first noticing how

[1] John x. 10.

exactly the terms employed to describe the two coincide, and then, how the means of establishing the two are the same, while in the course of the investigation we observe what new interpretations are given to the idea of the kingdom, by regarding it as eternal life.

I. Just as we saw that the kingdom of God was described as *come and yet coming*, as a dream of future realisation and yet a fact of realised experience, and just as we got at the meaning of the kingdom by studying this paradox ; so it is possible to quote two strings of sayings which intertwine in these Johannine discourses, the one establishing that the eternal life is future, the other that it is present.

1. It is future. *Whosoever drinketh the water that I shall give him shall never thirst; but the water that I shall give him shall become in him a well of water springing up unto eternal life.*[1] *Work not for the meat which perisheth, but for the meat which abideth unto eternal life.*[2] *He that reapeth receiveth wages and gathereth fruit unto eternal life.*[3] *He that hateth his life in this world shall keep it unto life eternal.*[4]

In such expressions eternal life is evidently a goal to be reached, a prize that is held out for future winning, a state of existence which lies beyond the range of the life that now is. But,

2. In other passages it is no less distinctly mentioned as something which already is here and now. *He that heareth my word and believeth Him that sent me hath eternal life.*[5] *This is the will of my Father,*

[1] John iv. 14.   [2] John vi. 27.   [3] John iv. 36.
[4] John xii. 25.   [5] John v. 24.

that every one that beholdeth the Son, and believeth on Him, have eternal life.[1] *He that believeth hath eternal life.*[2] *He that eateth my flesh and drinketh my blood hath eternal life.*[3] Nay, so truly is it a gift of the present that its possession will save a man from even seeing death.[4] *I give unto them eternal life, and they shall never perish, and no one shall snatch them out of my hand.*[5] *Whosoever liveth and believeth on me shall never die.*[6]

Here there is the same significant paradox which we discovered in our study of the kingdom of God. Eternal life is at once a future promise and a gift now received. Impossible as it is—the very word shows it—to confine eternal life to this life which now is; the life which now is, according to the thought of Jesus, is, or may become, the eternal life. To miss this point is to miss just what is most distinctive in His teaching. When we push the kingdom of God into the future world, and forget that the kingdom of God is among us already; and when we mean by eternal life the life of heaven, and ignore the meaning of the saying *He that believeth hath eternal life;* we are adopting the mode of thought which divides between this world and the world to come, and by so doing introduces a fatal unreality into the teaching of the Gospel.

It occurs to me that there is an illustration in literature of this peculiarity in the teaching of Jesus

[1] John vi. 40 : The *present* force of ἵνα ἔχῃ is lost in our English translation, as well as the implied contrast or addition in the next clause : "And I will raise him up at the last day."
[2] John vi. 47.   [3] John vi. 54.   [4] John viii. 51.
[5] John x. 28.   [6] John xi. 26.

concerning the eternal life, or kingdom of God, which may give the reader a fresh grasp of the thought underlying the words of Jesus. The first great Christian poet, Dante, wrote about Hell, Purgatory, and Heaven in so realistic a way, that no one can avoid recognising his conviction that in the life to come there are the states which He graphically describes. But, as Lowell has pointed out, the careful reader of the *Divina Commedia* is constantly reminded that the poet, in the middle course of his life, in that dismal wood of the exile, in his descent *ad inferos* and his return thence, desires to indicate that the scenes he paints are not future, but present. The imagery points not to departed spirits in a world beyond, but to spirits who were the poet's contemporaries, many of them actually alive when he wrote, occupying their several stations in Hell or Purgatory or Paradise. This is no fanciful conjecture of a commentator. Dante expressly says in the *Convito*, "Wicked men may be called truly dead." His intention is to bring home to the conscience that we are all now in this life either in Hell, or passing through Purgatory to Paradise, or in the Heaven of the Blessed already. Thus, Dante sees Frate Alberigo in the Inferno, though he was not dead. And in the description of Branca d'Oria, whom he meets in Hell, he gives this truly terrific touch: "He still eats and drinks and puts on clothes."

Certainly the poet had no intention of discrediting the popular idea that the dead passed into a world such as he depicted. Quite the contrary; with a sincere conviction he utters the theological teaching of his day. But just because he was a seer and not a systematiser in theology, just by his own vivid and penetrating power of piercing below the surface of things, he was led to give an actual meaning to a speculative dogma. Not only was he "the man who had been in hell" as the astonished people said; but he was the man who had shown hell, and heaven too, to be in the actual world of experience; the man who showed in what sense all men were in heaven or hell.

Now in this suggestion, which the modern reader cannot fail to see in the poem, Dante has caught the idea of Jesus. A great poet breaks through the cobwebs of ecclesiastical dogma. In the understanding of Jesus, His significance, His meaning, His methods, the poets often carry the palm.

Thus all through the fourth Gospel the conviction settles itself upon the reader that *eternal life*, though expressed in terms of duration, and referred to a future, is an actual possession in time. The kingdom of God is among us, since Jesus has been among us. The eternal life is within us, when we have believed on Him. Examine His words carefully and you find that Jesus knows nothing of an eternal life in the future for those of us who have it not in the present. By *eternal* He means "belonging to an order which does not, like this transitory world, pass away." The life He gives is of that order. He does not promise it as a future possession but He offers it for present acquisition. We do not wake into eternity after death. We are re-born into eternity now, and death becomes a negligible

P

quantity. That is the thought which sounds, like the trumpet of the last day, through the discourses of Jesus : " You men, in these fields of time and space, you now and here are living or dead. I offer you life—you live. You refuse it—you die. The last day is simply the ratification of To-day, eternity the expansion of Now."

II. But we may now pause to consider for a moment what further interpretation is given to the idea of the kingdom of God by the employment of the synonymous *eternal life*, and by the things which Jesus says about this life. We shall find that we are immediately led on to some vital and invaluable additions, and shall appreciate the wisdom of Jesus in not confining Himself to the earlier term.

In the Synoptic Gospels the kingdom of God was the subject of the preaching of Jesus. But, though His personality came more and more into prominence, He did not connect Himself with the Kingdom of God in any other way than that of the divinely-appointed herald and exponent of it. When, in the fourth Gospel, eternal life is presented as the equivalent of the kingdom, it is much more than the subject of His proclamation. It becomes His personal production in a direct and peculiar sense. *As the Father hath life in Himself,* He says, *even so gave He to the Son also to have life in Himself,*[1] so that as an original fount of life He could impart it to whom He would. *This is life eternal, to know Thee, the only true God, and Jesus Christ whom Thou hast sent.*[2] So that the kingdom

[1] John v. 26.   [2] John xvii. 3.

of God is in this new light to be found through a personal knowledge of God—as Father and Son— of the Father sending the Son into the world. Nay, we are carried further, and introduced into a region of singular mystery and power by the statement that He not only gives the life, but He *is* the life He imparts.[1] Using the simple image of the food by which the body is sustained, He announces Himself as *the bread of God which cometh down out of heaven, and giveth life unto the world.*[2] Or using the equally familiar image of water, He says: *If any man thirst, let him come unto me and drink:*[3] *whosoever drinketh of the water that I shall give him shall never thirst.*[4]

Even in the first mode of presentation it was evident that it would be vain to preach the kingdom of God to a world which would not have Him to reign over them, unless there should be some power to effect a change in the world's desire, and to engage the hearts of men to the obedience of His will. But only when this new idea was employed did it appear evident that Jesus had come with a miraculous power, which He could communicate, to transform the affections and the aims of men; that He was, indeed, not a King only, not a Teacher only, not a victim offered on an altar only, but Himself an immediate principle of supernatural life, that would effect an entrance into every willing heart, and there work out the moral and spiritual birth to which He gave the name, eternal

---

[1] John xiv. 6.
[2] John vi. 33.
[3] John vii. 37.
[4] John iv. 14.

life. *The hour cometh and now is*, He said, showing by the *now is* that He referred to a present spiritual resurrection, and not to the resurrection of the body at the last day, *when the dead shall hear the voice of the Son of God, and they that hear shall live.*[1]

It was, therefore, more than was implied even in the beautiful image of light; *I am the Light of the world:*[2] *the light is come into the world:*[3] *I am come a light into the world, that whosoever believeth on me may not abide in darkness.*[4] It is more even than was implied in the splendid saying, *The glory which Thou hast given me, I have given unto them.*[5] More than illumination, or instruction, more than dazzling revelations of the eternal verities, He offered Himself to be the transforming and sustaining life of those who believe in Him, as direct a nourishment to the soul of His disciple as the stock of the tree is to the branch.[6] And it is in view of this immediate and actual operation of Jesus on the soul that we must interpret His use of the word salvation. *Salvation was of the Jews;*[7] for He was every inch a Jew. *I say these things that ye may be saved,*[8] He exclaims, after one of His proudly humble self-assertions. *By me, if any man enter in, he shall be saved.*[9] *I came not to judge the world, but to save the world,*[10] yes, literally to impart Himself as the life to the dead and dying world.

[1] John v. 25. [2] John viii. 12. [3] John iii. 19,
[4] John xii. 46. [5] John xvii. 22. [6] John xv. 1, &c.
[7] John iv. 22. [8] John v. 34. [9] John x. 9.
[10] John xii. 47.

Are we not justified then in speaking of this teaching as *the roof of the building?* If the richly coloured and attractive sayings of the Synoptics had stood alone, we should have seen the fair proportions of the kingdom of God, as a city in the heavens, an ideal lying remote as a dream beyond our reach. But here comes the crowning truth. This is eternal life; the kingdom of God is the actual communication of the Person of Jesus, that stainless eternal Person, to the believing soul. With this the city comes down out of Heaven to the earth. Everything is practical, direct, supernatural. On the squared wall is set the covering roof.

III. And now to return to another evidence of the identity of the kingdom and the life, which reminds us that the eternal life is only an explanation and application of the kingdom of God: precisely the same means which we saw were to be employed for the establishment of salvation in the Kingdom of God are expressly detailed as the means of communicating eternal life, though of course with that greater stress laid on the Person of Christ which dictated the use of this more spiritual mode of statement:

1. Here, as in the first Gospels, the constant and never antiquated method of bringing life is preaching, *my word* or *words.* Jesus has the words of eternal life.[1] *If ye abide in my word, then are ye truly my disciples; and ye shall know the truth, and the truth shall make you free.*[2] *He that heareth my*

[1] John vi. 68.   [2] John viii. 32.

word, and believeth Him that sent me, hath eternal life.[1] On the other hand, *he that receiveth not my sayings hath one that judgeth him; the word that I spake, the same shall judge him in the last day.*[2] *Already ye are clean because of the word which I have spoken unto you.*[3] *If my words abide in you ask whatsoever ye will and it shall be done unto you.*[4] And so He protests to the Father: *The words which Thou gavest me I have given unto them.*[5] And it was the view of His mission which He presented to Pilate that He was born to bear witness unto the Truth,[6] which would refer primarily to His words. Indeed, the peculiar importance which He attaches to His own words and commandments in these deepest and most solemn of His discourses may give us a new ardour in prosecuting the study of His teaching.

2. Here, too, as has been already observed at some length, the Person of Jesus is brought into prominence as the means of effecting eternal life; so much so that He not obscurely hints that to reject Him is to surrender all hope of Life.[7] The variety of images which He employs, the bread, the water, the wine, lends a singular emphasis to the idea that it is after all not merely a teaching, a statement of truth, which saves, but, in the last resort, a creative act, parallel in the spiritual world to that which in the physical sphere forms and educes the human embryo as a living soul. Jesus

[1] John v. 24.   [2] John xii. 48.   [3] John xv. 3.
[4] John xv. 7.   [5] John xvii. 8.   [6] John xviii. 37.
[7] John xii. 47.

very explicitly states that in this process there is a mystery which it would be idle for Him to attempt to explain. One could almost fancy that a familiar passage in which He draws the parallel between *earthly* and *heavenly* things of this kind[1] once contained a suggestion, that, as the emergence of a living organism, though it is a purely earthly thing, remains an insoluble enigma, so the birth of the invisible spiritual organism baffles all inquiry. Perhaps He wishes to suggest that as both are beyond analysis, and yet the one is the most certain fact of all, we may rest content to recognise the other as a fact though it is impossible to investigate the mode of its production. No study of the processes relieves us of the wonder which swathes the origin of physical life. How the germ grows up into a man, or indeed what the germ is, must to all appearance go observed for ever, and never explained.

And in the same way the approach of Jesus to the soul through the simple gateway of an urgent faith, creates a new spiritual organism, of a piece and of a quality with His own. But who can tell how ? If He was silent, who shall even pretend to explain ?

3. Finally, the identification of Eternal Life with the kingdom of God in the earlier teaching is verified by the supreme method, which in each case was recognised as the indispensable condition of securing the object. The kingdom could not be established, as we saw, unless He who announced it, as the

[1] John iii. 12.

servant of all, should give His life a ransom for many. The thought of the promised realisation of the kingdom of God was intimately connected in His mind with the new covenant in His own blood.[1] And just in the same way, His death, throughout these discourses of John, presents itself to Him as the sole means of securing eternal life for men. *As Moses lifted up the serpent in the wilderness, even so must the Son of Man be lifted up that, whosoever believeth on Him should not perish but have eternal life.*[2]

Far more perceptibly than in the earlier teaching —as if St. John read back into all Jesus had said, the interpretation of the cross—there throbs through the discourses of this Gospel the heart-moving conviction in the spirit of Jesus: " To give eternal life to the world I must die." It becomes impressive not by any detailed explanation of the mystery; which, indeed, He never attempts to give; but by the stress and constant energy of His own thought in this direction. Death looms before Him as the significant method of victory, the purchase of the boon which the whole world wants.

The examination of this all-important point we must remit to a section by itself. But in closing the study of the kingdom of God, interpreted as eternal life, it is worth while to hint at a contrast between the teaching of Jesus and the noblest ethical ideal of antiquity. The Stoics taught that the wise man was a king, who by a sovereign control of his own passions and desires, and by a

[1] Luke xxii. 18–20.   [2] John iii. 16.

sublime self-poised indifference to the vulgar ambitions and adulations of others, might be said to rule his own realm in imperturbable security. The wise man thus drew apart from the world in a lofty and almost self-worshipping isolation. This was, I repeat, the most dignified and inspiring conception of life which the great speculative thinkers of the ancient world were able to form.

Jesus presented Himself as the striking contrast of this ideal, meek and lowly in heart. So far from encouraging men to be kings, He refused the title Himself. The only kingship He recognised was the subduing sovereignty of God in the heart, and the isolation of Stoicism, so far from being admired, was emphatically condemned. As all must be subjects of the heavenly King they must be drawn together in the heavenly commonwealth. And as the life so determined was imparted by His own personal contact with each, all would be like the limbs of one body, the branches of one tree. In a word, the final thought of ancient philosophy was a disintegrating individualism. The solidarity of a new humanity in the supernatural body of Jesus, the Son of God, was the message of the New Faith.

THE DEATH OF JESUS

JOHN xv. 13.

WE have repeatedly in these studies of the teaching of Jesus been forced to a conviction that a choice has to be made between His view of matters, and the view which has been subsequently taken, even by the greatest of His followers. Inspiration itself is never permitted to produce in any man the full-orbed rightness, and the complete immunity from extravagance, which characterise the Master's own teaching even when we see it only in fragments.

Such a choice we are compelled to make when we are considering the Death of Jesus. It was a subject which must have constantly engaged His attention. Whenever He speaks of it, He conveys an impression of having long brooded upon the mystery. His utterances, brief and pregnant, reveal in a shadowy way the conception which had filled His mind. But certainly there is a contrast between the death as it shapes itself to Him, and the death as it is reported and explained in the several theologies which have been constructed during the Christian ages. The contrast is partially concealed by our inveterate habit of first imposing on the thought of Jesus the interpretations contained elsewhere in the New Testament, and then imposing on the thought of the New Testament itself the views of later speculation. It is, therefore, a difficult task to isolate the ideas of Jesus, and to think of His death simply from His own point of view. But when we succeed in doing so, we become aware that not even John and Paul *fully* apprehended His thoughts, while all subsequent interpreters have been hampered by the supposed necessity of approaching His ideas only through the interpretations of these and the other Apostles.

Perhaps we should turn back to the section in which we examined what was said in the Synoptics on the subject; and then we can take up these more intimate discourses to see what further light they shed upon it. The agreement between the two sources is manifest both in what is said and in what is omitted. In the one, as in the other, He makes it plain that His death was necessary in order that He should accomplish the salvation of the world, which He had in view. It was not to Him a mere incident which was involved in the course lying before him; it was an essential, a central, part of the course itself. But, if possible, even less here than in Matthew and Luke does He offer us an explanation of that insoluble mystery, why, in what way, the death was the efficient cause of the result. Curiosity is evidently not to be gratified. We are brought into one of those very numerous regions of the divine action, where the processes can be recognised, appreciated, and accepted, but never explained. One thing, however, is immediately evident. Certain ideas which have played a great part in human doctrines of the Atonement, are not only absent, but precluded; and especially the idea which has effected a separation between the Father and the Son, and represented the suffering Son as offering a propitiation to the vengeful ire of the Father. If a phrase or two from St. Paul can be misquoted to establish that monstrous doctrine, at least it can find no foothold in any saying of Jesus. Now, if our views of Scripture and revelation forbid us to confine the doctrine of the Atonement to what Jesus has Himself presented on the subject; if we have reason to think that the Apostles were divinely commissioned to amplify and interpret what He said; if we are dissatisfied with the position that we have here a mystery which defies explanation, and claim in consequence for theology the right of constructing a speculative and rational scheme of the means by which Redemption is secured; we shall yet admit that His own thought on the subject should be considered first, that He who speaks from heaven may be heard before those who speak from earth; and we may, at least, demand as the touchstone of every theory which the thought of theologians may suggest, that it shall not be allowed at any point to contravene any expressed idea of Jesus.

If even this last very modest plea is sustained, many of the dismal *theologumena* which have distressed our childhood, and exasperated our maturer judgment, will quietly melt away and be forgotten.

We will approach, therefore, the consideration of His teaching about His own death in St. John's Gospel. And perhaps we shall obtain a clearer impression if we recognise that there were two stages in the doctrine. In the first instance there is the profound and deepening conviction that His death is necessary; in the second, there is a more specific realisation of the power which inflicts it, and the issues involved in the infliction.

I. There was a deep-laid conviction in the mind of Jesus that by dying He would reach men and save them, as it would not be possible to do if He shrank from the ordeal and the transformation of death. *Verily, verily I say unto you, except a grain of wheat fall into the earth and die, it abideth by itself alone; but if it die it beareth much fruit.*[1] Here was the idea that by dying He could multiply Himself, and arise out of the earth, not an isolated seed, but a rich harvest of souls. Elsewhere He exhibited the necessity of death under another image. Regarding Himself as the spiritual bread which could give life to men, He felt that an indispensable preliminary of supplying the nourishment was that He should be as it were ground in the mills of death *I am the living bread which came down out of heaven, if any man eat of this bread he shall live for ever; yea, and the bread which I will give is my flesh for the life of the world.*[2] The same thought of course underlies the image of the blood: *He that eateth my*

[1] John xii. 24.   [2] John vi. 51.

flesh and drinketh my blood, abideth in me, and I in him.[1] For as it is impossible to drink the blood of an animal unless it is shed, so evidently in the thought of Jesus, the world could not get the personal benefit of His life-giving power, and inward regeneration, unless He should consent to die. And considering the occasion on which He employed the analogy of the vine—viz., the eve of His death—perhaps we are justified in surmising that in His mind lurked the image of the tree, clipped, stripped and pruned, until it would appear as a dead stock in the ground, as a condition of a rich crop in the time of grapes.[2]

He felt it was expedient for Him to withdraw from the world as a human, fleshly being; because only so could He return as a life-giving Spirit. And thus the burden of that last discourse was that He must die and be lifted up, that He must be glorified through death, before the Comforter could come. "The Holy Spirit was not yet given because that Jesus was not yet glorified," says the evangelist.[3] To approach the world in any widely diffused, omnipresent, personal sense, implied that as a being limited in space and time He should cease to be.

It is not necessary for us to attempt a distinction between what theology has called "the second and third persons of the Trinity;" for Jesus does not anywhere sanction the kind of speculation out of which these definitions grow. But it is, rather necessary for us to observe that He does not distinguish between the coming of the Comforter and

---

[1] John vi. 56. [2] John xv. 1-8. [3] John vii. 39.

His own personal return to abide and operate in the world. So far from labouring to distinguish between the Son and the Spirit, the concern of Jesus is rather to identify them. Thus, when He has declared that in answer to His prayer the Father will give to the disciples *another Comforter* that shall be with them for ever, *even the Spirit of truth*,[1] He immediately adds, *I will not leave you desolate; I come unto you.*[2] The promise, *I will manifest myself to him,*[3] is not distinguished from the approach of the Comforter. And after all the detailed description of the Spirit's work, leading into truth, recalling what has been said, taking the things of Christ and showing them to men, He sums up the whole by saying, *A little while and ye behold me no more, and again a little while and ye shall see me.*[4]

Just as we saw that He declared to His judges that "from now ye shall see me coming in the clouds," so He categorically assured His disciples that from the time of His departure through death— and for that reason He joyfully incurred death—they should behold Him exalted and drawing all men to Him. And He discouraged them from expecting any apocalypse or outward manifestation, rather implying that through the Spirit He would Himself be pervasively present, working powerfully on the hearts of men, convincing the world of sin, of righteousness, and of judgment.

All this was the true and constantly avowed purpose of His mission; to save men He had come

---

[1] John xiv. 16.
[2] John xiv. 18.
[3] John xiv. 21.
[4] John xvi. 16.

into the world; and this was the way of saving them. His teaching must be carried home in order to affect and transform the heart. Not left to rumour, or repetition, or dogma, it must have an immediate and personal approach to the soul, operating upon it as a creative force. And for this purpose He saw that His death was an indispensable step. So long as He was there in the flesh He was limited; beyond the portal of death He would be emancipated. As therefore the everywhere operating means of communicating eternal life to men, and of establishing the kingdom of God in an actual reign over their hearts, it was essential that He should become spirit, and cease to be "flesh and blood."

This necessity was, as we have seen, constantly before the mind of Jesus. But evidently, if this were all, there remained a possibility, which, though the facts have rendered it almost unthinkable, was open to the power of God. For the mere purpose of commencing a world-wide operation through a spiritual agency, it was only necessary that He should pass out of the present conditions of time and space in some such way as story declared that Enoch and Elijah had done. It would have sufficed, if, at the appropriate time Jesus had gone up on high, leaving the vesture of His mortality, and had assumed His exalted station at the right hand of God. On the supposition of His nature being such as we saw it in previous sections to be there was no need for Him to die, in order to resume the spiritual condition which was naturally His. Supposing that death is the mere termination of a prescribed course

Q

to a human organism; this spirit, so little implicated in the mere fleshly organism, could have very easily slipped the leash and secured its freedom, either before, or with, the natural decay of the body. Supposing that death is to be regarded ethically as a penalty of sin, there was obviously no necessity for Him to die; because He had not sinned.

In any case, for the accomplishment of the work which is described in John xiv.–xvii. as the work of the Comforter, there is no *primâ facie* reason for, and in the character and career of Jesus there is every reason against, the awful humiliation, the lonely agony, the contumelious cross, the passage through the corruptions of the grave. All these factors, faithfully described in the narrative, and frankly accepted in the mind of Jesus, demand an explanation. He must have had an explanation of them. Emphatic, therefore, and repeated as is His thought, that His death was demanded as a means of His glorification and of His return to operate in the world under spiritual conditions alone, evidently this is not all. He has something else to say about His death. He has a mode of regarding it which exalts it to a more unique position than that of an episode in a long process of self-emptying, incarnation, and resurrection. He looks into the death itself and sees there an actual, indispensable sacrifice, by which, and, we should gather, by the special circumstances and details of which, a particular result was accomplished. And that result was the salvation of the world.

II. This specific, though mysterious, purpose of

the death is suggested in the discourse about the good shepherd,[1] who surrenders his life to the wolves in order to spare his flock. The image itself does not carry us very far; for evidently if the wolves succeeded in killing the shepherd the sheep would easily become their prey. And the image is indeed surrendered almost as soon as it is used; because Jesus says:[2] *I lay down my life that I may take it again.* This has at once carried us into a region of thought very far removed from the illustration of the shepherd.

It is therefore our duty to set aside the mere imagery, and to make an endeavour to follow the thought of Jesus, which swells and heaves, throwing up image after image, like crested waves on the surface, but is always far deeper and larger than any image which it employs. Here is the clear assertion that His death spares His disciples from a fate which otherwise would overwhelm them. If Jesus had not died they would have perished. And as the mere physical death does not come into consideration with Him, this is equivalent to saying: If the agony and passion of the cross had not been, men would have fallen victims to the spiritual destruction, which, in the case of Jesus, could only touch the body, because there was nothing in Him besides on which it could feed.[3]

This death He does not regard as inflicted by the Father. On the contrary the Father loves Him because He lays down His life. Nay, strange to say, He does not admit that any agent is responsible

[1] John x. 11-18.   [2] John x. 17.   [3] John xiv. 30.

for it, but distinctly asserts: *I lay down my life; no one taketh it away from me, but I lay it down of myself.*[1] With this simple statement vanish all notions of the Father inflicting death on the Son, of the human instruments being anything more than the occasion of the death, and of the malign powers of evil obtaining any victory over Jesus for a moment. Rather He distinctly claims that it is a voluntary offering: its value lies in its spontaneity. *The Prince of this world cometh, and he hath nothing in me; but that the world may know that I love the Father, and as the Father gave me commandment, even so I do.*[2]

It is a sheer act of love and obedience. Wrath, violence, vengeance, retaliation, and all the dismal passions which men so easily imagine, because they so easily entertain, have here not so much as a foothold.

But in the mention of that shadowy form *The Prince of the World* we seem to have a clue. On another occasion, when a heavenly voice had declared that the name of Jesus had been and should yet further be glorified, Jesus said, *Now is the judgment of this world: now shall the Prince of this world be cast out. And I, if I be lifted up from the earth, will draw all men unto myself.*[3] Here, as in the Synoptics, emerges the idea of a personal and malignant power of evil, who has established an ascendancy over the human race; and that ascendancy seems to be broken, first, by the fact that he finds nothing in Jesus but a sinless human being, but secondly, by

[1] John x 18. [2] John xiv. 30, 31. [3] John xii. 31, 32.

that sharp death-conflict in which Jesus engages. The self-offering which is so profoundly gratifying to the Father—*for their sakes I consecrate myself*, probably as a sacrifice, *that they may be consecrated in truth*[1]—is a blow to the Prince of the world, which breaks his spell over men. For, observe, the narrative of Christ washing the disciples' feet,[2] covers the saying in Matthew: *the Son of Man came not to be ministered unto but to minister*, and this saying about His self-consecration covers the concluding clause, *and to give His life a ransom for many*.

The voluntary offering of love and obedience on the cross, broke, it would seem, the power of that malignant foe that leads men captive at his will.

It is rather surprising that there is nothing in the fourth Gospel which corresponds to the *blood shed for the remission of sins* in Matthew; nor is there any attempt to suggest that the divine forgiveness waited on that sacrifice of the cross. But this is not enough to justify Beyschlag in treating the clause *for the remission of sins* as a spurious insertion in the older source. For in the Johannine writings, which are suffused with the *thought* of Jesus, just as they suffuse the teaching of Jesus with their peculiar terminology, we have not only " Behold the Lamb of God, which taketh away the sin of the world,"[3] which is general, but the particular statements, " The blood of Jesus His Son cleanseth us from all sin, and He is the propitiation for our sins, and not for ours only, but also for the whole world."[4]

---

[1] John xvii. 19.
[2] John xiii. 1-11.
[3] John i. 29.
[4] 1 John i. 7, ii. 2.

If, therefore, Jesus abstains from specifically connecting His death in these discourses with the forgiveness of sins, we may surmise that it is not because He repudiates that idea; which certainly colours the very source itself; but rather because He did actually on the eve of the crucifixion direct our thoughts to a more inclusive conception of His death. If His blood was to be shed for the remission of sins, and if intrinsically the free forgiveness of the Father which He announced depended upon that consecrated offering, it was in virtue of this larger significance of the conflict, that His death effected a positive victory over the one power which was binding men in misery and iron, and ransomed, not a few only, but the whole world[1] from the cruel tyranny of the foe.

Confining ourselves, therefore, as closely as we can to His own language in this Gospel, we find the situation shaping itself to our eye in the following way. The world, that is, the scene of human freedom, lies in the power of an enemy who holds tyrannical sway over souls; and in the spiritual sense, as far as souls can be said only to *live* in the love and obedience of God, this enemy slays them as ravening wolves harry and destroy a helpless flock. Jesus, entering the world, the arena where this spiritual rebel exercises an obvious supremacy, became in all points a man, and took upon Himself all the conditions over which the foe had triumphed. But Jesus held Himself entirely aloof from this power of the world, and never admitted so much as

[1] 1 John ii. 2.

a breath of the evil to penetrate Him. And in that sense even before His death He could say: *be of good cheer, I have overcome the world.*[1]

But He saw—and this is the point which He leaves unexplained, the point of mystery which defies every effort to penetrate—that if He exposed His innocent life to the unchecked onslaught of this malevolent power; if without taking refuge in any divine prerogatives, or screening body or soul against the subtle and exasperated attacks, He would resolutely face the consequences; though He would die apparently under the execration of the world, numbered among its transgressors, indistinguishable from the criminals on whom falls the vengeance of men and God; a supremely redemptive result would follow. He would of course rise again; He knew that it was impossible for death to hold Him; the experience could, from the nature of the case, be only a sharp and desperate crisis: but by that brief and awful passage through death, that inward wrestle, the meaning of which could be discovered to the observer only by a few outward signs, He saw that He could overthrow the enemy, and obtain a victory over the world which would apply not to His own person only, but potentially to the whole race with which He had identified Himself. The thought which led Him on, and rendered Him inflexible, which set His face like a flint, and armed that exquisite soul with the endurance of adamant, was just that which obtains such various expression all through the discourses of St. John. There was a

[1] John xvi. 33.

great joy set before Him. If He consecrated Himself in this act of unstinted sacrifice, if He did not fail in the mysterious furnace to do His part, the part which only He could do, the result would be that henceforth whosoever believed on Him would enter into His victory, would escape the bondage that is in the world through lust, would receive an actual divine pardon, based on eternal principles of right, and would enter into His glory, which, through the cloud of sin, thus shone bright upon a ransomed world.[1]

That being the essential thought, present we may surmise to Him, but never explicable to our minds, which see only from the human side, it was as it were only a derived result, that being thus lifted up, He would draw all men to Him by the most powerful appeal of a sacrifice unto death. *Greater love hath no man than this, that a man lay down his life for his friends.*[2] It is not enough to say that the exhibition of such love works a saving result on the believer, because indeed the love which works the result is already the love which has made this vast unfathomable sacrifice. While we are merely regarding Jesus as one who suffers death, a martyr for truth, slain by the malignity of prejudiced and unprincipled men, there is much to move admiration and even

---

[1] I may observe that Dr. Dale's last utterance to the world on the Atonement in his invaluable book *Christian Doctrine*, suggests a very interesting rationale of the sacrifice of Christ, on the lines of his famous book on the subject. But I could not possibly adopt it here, because evidently it has no point of connection with the Teaching of Jesus Himself.

[2] John xv. 13.

provoke imitation, but there is as yet nothing to produce a love capable of transforming a sinful heart. This love is only produced when we apprehend that the death was not a mere human death, and was not inflicted, intrinsically, by men at all, but was, as Jesus Himself has explained, a perfectly voluntary offering, inward and spiritual rather than merely corporeal; a passionate, intense conflict with the Power of Sin, which it is never possible for us to fathom; a sacrifice, therefore, of an incalculable value which He made as the indispensable condition of securing our salvation.

It is this, as doubtless He foresaw, which provokes the intense and transforming love of the sheep for the Shepherd who died.

We seem therefore to be moving along the track of His own thought most closely when we conceive the death on the cross as a mighty conflict with the power of evil which enslaves and ruins the world, a conflict which through apparent defeat achieved an actual triumph ; the supreme and crowning example of the struggle between darkness and light, between life and death, which appears to continue throughout the drama of temporal history, but is predetermined in its issue, the victory never being really doubtful. The death and resurrection of Jesus are at once a witness and a guarantee of the victory which is to come.

> From morn to eve they struggled—Life and Death,
>   At first it seemed to me that they in mirth
>   Contended, and as foes of equal worth,
> So firm their feet, so undisturbed their breath.

But when the sharp red sun cut through its sheath
Of western clouds, I saw the brown arm's girth
Tighten and bear that radiant form to earth,
And suddenly both fell upon the heath.

And then the wonder came; for when I fled
To where those great antagonists down fell,
I could not find the body that I sought,
And when and where it went I could not tell;
One only form was left of those who fought,
The long dark form of Death—and it was dead.[1]

[1] Mr. Cosmo Monkhouse's magnificent sonnet, one of the greatest, in my opinion, of this century, does not explicitly refer to the great theme of the Passion on the Cross in connection with which it is quoted. But, like all great poetry, it is greater than it knows. Entering into one of the most moving thoughts of human existence, it tracks it up, unconsciously, to the most moving instance of the thought. And presumably treating only of the passing of a human soul, it lays bare the significance of that most momentous passing of the most momentous soul—the death of Jesus.

THE COMMUNITY OF BELIEVERS

JOHN xvii. 20, 21

IN this Gospel of St. John, which not only contains the fulness of the teaching of Jesus, but also marks the highwater line of New Testament thought, the word *Church* does not occur at all. The word which takes its place is *Love*. It is on the same principle that the kingdom of God is translated into eternal life, or repentance and forgiveness of sin appear as new birth. There is an attempt made to get at the essence of the idea, and to avoid any merely external characterisation of it. Now a Church is, as the event has proved, comparatively easy to make and maintain, while love is always difficult. Yet where love is not, the Church ceases; and, on the other hand, where the new commandment is accepted and obeyed, where we love one another as Christ has loved us, there is His Church. Men are always anxious to define the Church beforehand by some easily produced marks, such as orders or sacraments. Jesus insists on defining it solely by love. *By this shall men know that ye are my disciples, if ye have love one to another.*[1] As He spoke all these deepest and

[1] John xiii. 35.

highest of His sayings without so much as mentioning the word, we also may avoid it. It is always better to approach His ideas in His own way. And it is remarkable that even now, as men become more truly Christian, and enter more deeply into the thought of this fourth Gospel, they use the word *Church* less and less, while *Love* becomes more and more the substitute for it.

In the great high-priestly prayer His thought is of those who believe on Him, and *them also that believe on me through their word; that they may all be one; even as Thou, Father, art in me, and I in Thee, that they also may be in us; that the world may believe that Thou didst send me.*[1] Union is to be sought and found through the personal faith of individual souls in Him. Accordingly the teaching in this Gospel gives a remarkable prominence to the act, and to the attitude —for the aorist and present tenses in the original clearly distinguish the two—of believing in Him. In the introduction of the Gospel a note is struck which vibrates throughout : As many as received Him, to them gave He the right to become children of God, even to them that believe on His name; which were born not of blood, nor of the will of the flesh, nor of the will of man, but of God.[2]

First comes the faith of each ; then follows the community of the faithful.

I. The individual *must be born again*. This is purposely presented at the outset, in chapter iii. Repentance and remission of sins, which were frequently mentioned in the Synoptics, here do not

[1] John xvii. 20, 21.   [2] John i. 12, 13.

occur at all. On the other hand that believing, which was seldom mentioned in the Synoptics except as the condition of physical healing, is here repeated again and again. Nor is it any more simply believing *in the Gospel*,[1] it is rather believing Jesus Himself. Faith is not so much the intellectual acceptance of the message as the personal trust in a Saviour.

This change of terminology is what one might expect. As we get into the core of the teaching of Jesus we find Him little disposed to deal with external things which may easily delude, but always pressing firmly and persistently on central and spiritual facts, which, in His view, are essential.

Repentance, forgiveness, conversion, these are processes which have an outward expression, and are defined as they strike an observer. They may easily be confused with external phenomena such as tears and beating on the breast, or the absolution uttered by a priest's lips, or a change of habit and demeanour. Though their essence is far from being merely formal, they may very easily be formal and even mechanical. But come to the centre and spring of these things, the unobservable element, which is yet the essence of the whole matter to consciousness, and what is it? It is a faith in Jesus of such a kind as produces an actual new birth; and that introduction of a new spiritual creation under the surface of a man's life is viewless and trackless as the passage of the wind.[2] There is a mystery which is incapable of further analysis or explanation. It is

[1] Mark i. 15. [2] John iii. 8.

the work of Jesus Himself, an operation of spirit upon the inward life of a man. Stated in this way it defies evasion. A man cannot say, " I have repented, or done acts of penance, I have received absolution and am forgiven, I am born again because I am baptised," and so cheat himself. For it is a matter of an inward spiritual change which is its own evidence, a birth within, no more doubtful than the original birth of the body into the world of sense. By this mode of speech Jesus has supplied a searching test. He has taken the criterion of religion out of the uncertainties and deadening delusion of external forms and placed it in the one region of certainty, consciousness itself. Equally clear is His assertion about the mode of the new birth. He definitely explains that it is produced by believing in Him.[1] *He that believeth on Him is not judged.*[2] Identifying the new birth, which is the commencement, with eternal life, which is the continuation, He says : *Verily, verily, I say unto you, He that believeth hath eternal life.*[3] *Believe in God, believe also in me.*[4] *While ye have the light believe on the light, that ye may become sons of light.*[5] To believe on Him is the efficient cause of a birth—" becoming sons of light "—a new birth of the Spirit. And this is so constantly emphasised that we may say : not only does the faith produce the new life, but where the faith is, the life has already begun in embryo, though it has not yet emerged into consciousness. Yes, in a sense, the new life may be said to start from the

[1] John iii. 15.   [2] John iii. 18.   [3] John vi. 47.
[4] John xiv. 1.   [5] John xii. 36.

exertion of the will in the direction of obedience to His word. *If any man willeth to do His will, he shall know of the teaching, whether it be of God.*[1] For, as distinct from the will of the flesh,[2] there is a will to believe in Jesus which is already the work of the Spirit, and the pledge of a completed birth which is to be.

This initial act of faith, the will to believe, the readiness to receive Jesus, so far as one sees, and to go on further, as understanding extends, which is in the Synoptics compared to a grain of mustard seed sure to grow, is pregnant with promise. For here Jesus likens it to the connection of a branch with the parent stock of the vine.[3] The act of faith has established a connection with Jesus, and the continuation of this act is equivalent to abiding in Him, as the branch abides in the vine. The sap which is not to be found in a severed branch, courses freely through the branch that is connected with the stock; and the characteristic fruit of the vine appears. The fruit is in this case the fulfilment of those commandments—those counsels of perfection—which were detailed in such discourses as the Sermon on the Mount. This realisation of the impossible commandments, a supernatural result of His own inworking, produces a singular relation of intimacy with Himself: *If ye keep my commandments ye shall abide in my love.*[4] And from this relation of love to Him follows a new commandment, which is not significant until the disciple is brought into this

---

[1] John vii. 17.
[2] John i. 13.
[3] John xv. 1.
[4] John xv. 10.

intimacy with his Lord: *This is my commandment, that ye love one another, even as I have loved you.*[1]

Here, like a veiled bride, the Church appears, unnamed.

Love was, as He says in the Synoptics, the fulfilling of the Law. And love is the outcome of this new life which is maintained by a personal faith in Him. And love will immediately produce a Church. *A new commandment I give unto you, that ye love one another; even as I have loved you, that ye also love one another. By this shall all men know that ye are my disciples if ye have love one to another.*[2]

But before we follow up this suggestion, we must pause for a moment to observe how this vital power of the new life operates in the individual believer.

It must be noted that there is no thought of substituting belief for action, or of setting *faith*, as St. Paul called it, against *works*. For here, as in the Synoptics, He says that the judgment of men will be according to their works. Men *shall come forth* from the tombs; *they that have done good unto the resurrection of life, and they that have done ill unto the resurrection of judgment.*[3] But a singularly hopeful turn is given to the thought. The thought in itself fills us with apprehension. It is well known that no one is easy in the expectation of being judged according to works, except those who to evil living have added the callousness of a dead conscience. They who have been the most worthy in the judgment of men are precisely those who shrink most sensitively from

[1] John xv. 12.   [2] John xiii. 34, 35.   [3] John v. 29.

standing on their merits in the judgment of God. But one saying of Jesus gives a new and quickening significance to the principle. "What shall we do that we may work the works of God?" was a question once put to Him. And He replied: *This is the work of God, that ye believe*—we might almost say, in order to render the force of the present tense, that ye live a life of faith—*in Him whom He hath sent*.[1] Here we are led to the very spring of a life which can be acceptable with God. It is not a life of striving by meritorious actions to secure a favourable verdict at the judgment, but it is a life of vital union by faith with Jesus Himself, a life in which all the results of holy living are wrought in the disciple by the constant and effective operation of the Master's supernatural influence.

Faith in Jesus is the power of an endless life; it is a love which fulfils the law; it is a security which defies the judgment.

And before we pass on let us observe that this faith is not the privilege of a few, but the opportunity presented to all. Though the broad and simple invitation, *Come unto me, all ye that labour*, is not repeated, Jesus implies again and again a perfect freedom of access for whosoever will come to Him. *They shall all be taught of God.* Nothing could be wider than this. *Every one that hath heard from the Father and hath learned, cometh unto me.*[2] The success of the call depends on the attention which is given to it. *Him that cometh to me I will in no wise cast out.*[3]

[1] John vi. 29.　　　[2] John vi. 45.　　　[3] John vi. 37.

In view of the small number who, to all appearance, accept the call it is possible, as we saw, to say, *Many are called but few are chosen.* But the language of Jesus, both here and in the Synoptics, forbids us to think of any favouritism. Rather our attention is turned to an inner fitness. They who love the light, they who love the truth, turn to Jesus, the light and the truth. They believe under the impulse of this inner affinity, drawn by the attraction which light and truth have for such souls. But every one might believe, and the same result would follow. *Whosoever will,* is the form of invitation.

II. Now they who believe form the community of Jesus. In contrast with *the world,* He calls them *those whom Thou hast given me.*[1]

It is of course a far simpler matter to fix on certain forms of ecclesiastical organisation, guaranteed by traditional observances, and to assert that all who maintain these observances and remain within the border of these forms belong to the Church of Jesus, good and bad, without regard to inward faith or spiritual conformity to His ideas. This course is so much simpler, and to human minds, with an impetuous demand for definiteness, so much more attractive, that it can occasion no surprise to find that it has been adopted. But the thought of Jesus is not only different, it is the precise opposite of this. His one concern is to establish only an inward and spiritual test. He is scrupulous, with a care which of itself might establish His superhuman wisdom, to avoid dropping

[1] John xvii. 9.

even one word which might encourage that external standard of judgment.

There is *the world* which He has come to save. He does not begin by capturing Judaism, or the empire, nations or institutions. His method is to call out individuals, those who believe on Him. This is His new flock, gathered from many folds. With the utmost delicacy He distinguishes between a fold, which is an external organisation, and a flock, which is an aggregate of individuals. There are many folds; His sheep are found in all; but there is one flock, one Shepherd;[1] that is, evidently, a flock, the unity of which is preserved only by a relation to the Shepherd. *The children of God are scattered abroad*,[2] *but it is His personality that gathers them together into one.*

It is a gross and obvious thought to make a Church in the human sense of the word, a community of persons united by outward observances, an institution which can take its place among the institutions of this world. But the idea of Jesus is all His own. He proposes to link together through the ages the souls that believe in Him, follow Him, and love Him, and are consequently drawn into a fellowship of imperishable love.

This fellowship of souls He referred to as the temple of His body.[3] From the moment of His resurrection this temple would begin to arise on the foundation of His death. Each soul, believing,

---

[1] John x. 16: The contrast between αὐλή, the equivalent of *Church* in the Catholic sense, and ποίμνη, the equivalent of *Church* in the spiritual sense, has never been sufficiently apprehended.

[2] John xi. 52.   [3] John ii. 19.

would be gathered to its appointed place in the spiritual structure. The image of the temple merges always into the image of the body. Each stone is a *lively* stone; each member of the body is *built* in by the master builder. But, if we may leave the images for a moment, His thought is this:—The spiritual community, which is formed by a personal faith in Himself, which is compacted together solely by this quick and effectual union with Him, forms, and will form for ever, an organism; and this organism is not only the final cause of His incarnation, but also the final cause of the creation of man. Jesus is a pure idealist, from the standpoint of earth; from the standpoint of heaven He is the only realist. All kingdoms, Churches, communities must pass away. His alone will survive.

He prayed that these members of His body should be one, in the same sense that He and the Father are one.[1] And that prayer has always been answered, for, as He said: *I know that thou hearest me always.*[2] Ever from the beginning there has been one flock, one shepherd. No *fold*, not even the Roman, has ever succeeded in parting the flock of Jesus. Baxter and Ken, Bunyan and Tillotson, yes, Howe and Stillingfleet, have always been one, one in Jesus. Even to-day, no doctrinaire theory was ever able to keep Dean Stanley or Phillips Brooks from the absolute and loving unity with the other sheep which were not of their fold. The intolerance of Romanism or Anglicanism is simply due to ignorance of the teaching of Jesus.

[1] John xvii. 21. [2] John xi. 42.

His flock, a gracious community of the Spirit, feeds in the verdant pastures and beside the still waters, and is hardly so much as aware of polemical journals and the denunciations of bigotry. All who are in Jesus are in His flock, nor can any be in His flock who are not in Him: *My sheep hear my voice, and I know them, and they follow me; and I give unto them eternal life; and they shall never perish, and no one shall snatch them out of my hand.*[1] The idea that He will reject those who have not been able to see a divine institution in episcopacy, or the mass, or the papacy, could never have been formed —or formed, could never be entertained—by any one who has with an exclusive obedience set himself to hear the voice of the Shepherd, and to seriously grasp what He means.

As the community of Jesus is spiritual so also is its worship. Sacred buildings have no significance. Everything turns on the worship being *in spirit and in truth.*[2] The only sacred building is the temple of His body. Jesus in His most intimate moods was very chary of even alluding to outward forms, knowing their peril. We saw that, while He would have nothing to say to sacred buildings, or ritual, He evidently did adopt two simple observances, baptism and the supper, as the symbols of His spiritual community. But, perhaps because already when John wrote the tendency to unduly emphasise these forms had appeared, this transcript from the inward thought of Jesus, the fourth Gospel, quietly drops all mention even of those simple observances. In

[1] John x. 27, 28.   [2] John iv. 21-24.

chapter iii. Jesus anticipates all error by explaining that a man cannot be regenerated by water alone; for *unless he is born of water and of the Spirit he cannot enter the kingdom of God.*[1] And that birth of the Spirit is, as we have seen, the inward result of a personal faith in Him. In the same way, though the scene in the upper chamber on the eve of His death is given at great length, all mention of the supper and its institution is omitted; while on the other hand, again, error is forestalled by the discourse in chapter vi., where Jesus shows that to eat His body and drink His blood is not a rite at all, but a deep inward assimilation of His spirit and His power. And with a divine prevision, in reference to this very discourse, He says: *The words which I have* (just) *spoken to you are spirit and are life.*[2] This mode of treatment is certainly not intended to discredit baptism and the Lord's supper; but just as certainly it for ever excludes the interpretation which is known as sacramentarianism.

This community, animated by the real presence of Jesus, has those extraordinary privileges and graces which, mentioned in the Synoptics, are here given in much fulness of detail. The hatred of the world,[3] and even active persecution,[4] are from the nature of the case inevitable. But this incidental feature almost disappears in the glory of the blessing, as the spots in the sun's disk are invisible when noon is ablaze.

To begin with, these who believe (not the world

[1] John iii. 5.
[2] John vi. 63: The insertion of "just" gives the force of the perfect tense, λελάληκα. [3] John xv. 18-20. [4] John xvi. 1-3.

of indifferent, formal, sceptical persons who are confounded with the community of Jesus) have the privilege to ask anything in His name, and to receive what they ask for: *Hitherto have ye asked nothing in my name; ask and ye shall receive that your joy may be full.*[1] Indeed their prayers for joy are anticipated by Him: *Now I come to Thee; and these things I speak in the world, that they may have my joy fulfilled in themselves.*[2] That joy is all inclusive and is of an unearthly order; in this world it appears like a ray of outer sunshine penetrating a dark room through the crevice of a shutter. And the outcome of this believing prayer is not only joy but peace: *Peace I leave with you, my peace I give unto you; not as the world giveth, give I unto you.*[3] For joy, even Christ's joy, would be an imperfect boon unaccompanied by peace, even Christ's peace.

> " Who are thy playmates, boy ? "
> " My favourite is Joy,
> Who brings with him his sister Peace to stay
>   The livelong day.
>   I love them both, but he
>   Is most to me."
>
> " And where thy playmates now,
>   O man of sober brow ? "
> " Alas! dear Joy, the merrier, is dead.
>   But I have wed
>   Peace; and our babe, a boy,
>   Newborn is Joy."[4]

---

[1] John xvi. 24.   [2] John xvii. 13.   [3] John xiv. 27.
[4] This exquisite little lyric by Mr. J. B. Tabb, possibly without his own intention, expresses the peculiar difference between Christ's joy and the merely human joy which we all so restlessly desire.

Joy and Peace. Yes, incredible as it must seem to those who confuse the Church of Christ with external institutions, and try to interpret *it* through polemical writings, it is a simple matter of fact that in the true Church, always and everywhere, through prosperity and adversity, in persecution as in rare moments of relief, joy and peace abide.

Perhaps, however, the supreme privilege and grace of this community is that its members are witnesses for Him.[1] Through them in the world the Spirit works, convicting and converting. Their mutual love marks them out as His disciples.[2] This supernatural love, maintained in the face of apparent impossibilities, convinces the world that God has sent Jesus.[3] Possibly if we all agreed in opinion, and all belonged to one fold, there would be nothing very superhuman in this love. But when men of different Churches and different opinions are united in Jesus, this affords a powerful testimony of His reality. And through their word others believe on Him.[4]

And although *they who had been with Him from the beginning,*[5] the first circle of apostles, had a peculiar witness to give, which could not fall to their successors—a witness, we may reverently believe, embodied for ever in these four Gospels— so that the community would rest on the apostles and prophets, Jesus Christ Himself being the chief corner stone, throughout the course of history; yet all who should believe through their word, as a

---

[1] John xv. 26, 27. [2] John xiii. 35. [3] John xvii. 21.
[4] John xvii. 20. [5] John xv. 27.

community of love and service, secure of His presence through the observation of His commandments, would have their appropriate witness to deliver, an apostolic succession, generation after generation.

And amongst other more material signs which would follow them that believe, should be one of a mysterious and inward nature. As, age after age, the Holy Spirit should breathe on this community of believers, their presence in the world would produce a threefold conviction, of sin and righteousness and judgment.[1] The regenerate community will be a perpetual charge of sin against those who do not believe in Jesus: a perpetual standard of righteousness, maintained by the presence of Jesus with them and with the Father; and a perpetual reminder of judgment, as it succeeds in wresting province after province from the Prince of this world.

And as this community should be knit together by the Spirit alone, and should depend only on spiritual means, it would, through that divine indwelling manifested by deed and word, not only "bind and loose" as we saw in the Synoptics, but forgive or retain the sins of men.[2] It was spoken not to the Twelve alone,[3] nor to any one individually, but to the disciples, as such, and the disciples as a community. We must believe that it is spoken to us in just the same sense, on just the same

---

[1] John xvi. 8.   [2] John xx. 23.
[3] See John xx., where the Twelve (verse 24) are distinguished from the body of disciples, verse 19.

terms, as it was to that first representative group. Do we receive the Holy Ghost? Is He in our Church community? Are His mighty powers experienced by us, and manifested in love and by all the other signs which Jesus has described? Then on us devolves the mysterious power which Jesus does not explain, which none of the apostles even ventured to explain: *Receive ye the Holy Ghost; whose soever sins ye forgive, they are forgiven unto them; whose soever sins ye retain, they are retained.*[1]

[1] John xx. 23: Every unbiassed student of the words of Jesus and of the Epistles (*e.g.*, 1 Cor. v. 3-5; 1 John v. 16) will observe that it is quite impossible to find any genuine foundation for what is called priestly absolution in the New Testament. The mysterious power given to the community of faith depends on an actual reception of the Holy Ghost; and nothing in Scripture or experience tends to show that episcopal ordination, as such, imparts the Holy Ghost to a man. To examine in detail the interpretations which have been suggested for this verse would lead us too far afield.

THE RESURRECTION

John xi. 25.

IT must by this time be clear to every reader that in order to understand Jesus it is necessary to surrender oneself to His teaching. It is all so original, so far removed from the beaten tracks of ordinary teachers, that to approach it with fixed presuppositions is most surely to misread it. This teaching has been given as the perpetual standard by which everything shall be tried: *He that rejecteth me, and receiveth not my sayings, hath one that judgeth him; the word that I spake, the same shall judge him in the last day.*[1] When, therefore, we take our own theories to His sayings for support rather than correction, using the standard which is to test simply as an argument to confirm the long errors of the ages, we expose ourselves to this severest of all judgments, that we have no longer any mode of arriving at truth; we are handed over blindfold to the mistakes of men.

Even in the Gospels themselves there are instances of preconceived ideas in the writers, slightly warping the words of Jesus; though happily the

[1] John xii. 48.

body of His undiluted sayings is so substantial that it is possible to supply the corrections. But the Church has so far lost the sense of His teaching and its significance that, without any attempt to understand it as a whole, she unblushingly singles out disconnected texts to support views of her own, which are the exact antithesis of His teaching when it is studied by itself in an unprejudiced way.

Now on no subject was it harder, as we saw before, to understand His ideas than on eschatology. When He spoke about the last things, death and judgment, and the final condition of the good and the evil, His hearers listened full of certain traditional ideas of their own. Language which He employed in His peculiar and penetrating way, they were apt to take in a conventional sense. They have preserved sufficient evidence that His thought was of startling originality; but they also furnish evidence that they constantly tended to reduce it to the mere commonplaces of Rabbinical dogma. Naturally enough every contracted and inadequate interpretation of the first hearers has been very dear to minds which are more eager to reach definite dogmatic statements than to assimilate the thought of Jesus.

The single expression, *I am the Resurrection*, at once reminds us that we have to do with a doctrine very far removed from those which appear both in Jewish and Christian systems of theology. For evidently it is not possible to tone down the phrase into *I shall rise again*, or *I shall raise others from the dead.* It is a peculiarly emphatic and quite unique utterance.[1]

Now just as Jesus turns the thought of Mary away from that remote and unknown resurrection to which we all so instinctively refer, and fixes her attention on the startling announcement, I AM; so it is clear to every careful reader of these discourses that He had a remarkable and original doctrine, that the resurrection is a present fact, that judgment is now proceeding, and the final condition of men is being from moment to moment decided. And it is, in His mode of speaking, rather as a background to these immediate and tangible realities, that the vision of resurrection, judgment, heaven and hell, as men popularly understand the terms, rises indeterminate and vague, as if purposely subordinated to the things of pressing moment.

It is a peculiar quality of His teaching to recall the wandering fancy, and bring it to the point. He never gratifies curiosity; but is always ready to answer the question, "What shall I do that I may inherit eternal life?" He finds us always eager to discuss the unknown, and to sketch schemes of eschatology; nothing do men love better than to launch away from the shore of ascertainable reality, and on the shifting seas to build their imaginary structures. But He rebukes the tendency. "That with which you are concerned," He always seems to be saying, "is here

---

[1] Ἐγώ εἰμι ἡ ἀνάστασις. Of course ἐγώ alone, or εἰμι alone would have expressed the idea. But ἐγώ lays stress on the person, and εἰμι on the actual and present fact.

before you. The pressing question is whether now you are risen from the dead. Why not judge your own selves now? Here is hell, close as the valley of Hinnom, which lies outside the city walls. Here also is eternal life for a man to possess and hold immediately." Not, of course, that He denies those ultimate things to which the whole creation moves; but He distinctly alters the centre of gravity. The unknown future is intimately connected with the present; and all interest is centred in the present. No man, holding fast to Christ's teaching, could fall into the delusion that life is to be passed in speculation about coming events, or in relegating everything of importance to the unseen world.

There are then two lines of His thought which have to be followed out, and it is important to attach to them the relative importance which He attaches. (*i*) There are the present realities which begin to exist from the time of His own presence in the world, and are to us all pressing as food and sleep are pressing for our bodies. These are the things with which alone we are vitally concerned. (*ii*) There are the shadowy results of the world's history, to which He frequently alluded, sometimes using popular forms of speech, sometimes flashing a light of His own upon them, but always making it clear that He does not wish us to speculate, or to go beyond what is written. *It is not for you to know*, is His formula.[1] His purpose is only to give us strong assurance that all will be well in the dark and mysterious night of death.

[1] Acts i. 7.

I. THE PRESENT REALITIES. (1) Resurrection. *Verily, verily, I say unto you,* He says, in His most impressive way, *the hour cometh and now is, when the dead shall hear the voice of the Son of God and they that hear shall live.*[1] It is not possible to refer this saying to the isolated miracle of the raising of Lazarus, partly because of the emphatic *and now is,* but partly also because the words follow close upon the wonderful assertion, *He that heareth my word and believeth Him that sent me, hath eternal life, and cometh not into judgment, but hath passed out of death into life.*[2] This connection must settle the interpretation. The miraculous resurrection of Lazarus was simply a symbol of a far more important truth than the mere restoration to an earthly life conveys. It was a visual illustration of a fact which is too inward and subtle to come under the eye of observers at all. The fact is this: that from the moment of vital faith in Jesus a resurrection-life begins in the soul, and this resurrection-life is of so predominant and masterly a character that the death of the body may be ignored. *He that liveth and believeth in me shall never die,*[3] He said, *This is the bread which cometh down out of heaven, that a man may eat thereof and not die.*[4] A bold utterance in a land where it was hard to tread without stepping on a tomb, and in a Church where for nineteen centuries the believers have shared the common lot, and have perished even more lamentably than the self-seeking world. But a paradox is the best of teachers, because it arrests attention.

---

[1] John v. 25. [2] John v. 24.
[3] John xi. 26. [4] John vi. 50.

This teaching about the resurrection is quite original. Other religions, and even Christianity through most of its official teachers, have confined the attention of men to a physical resurrection in the future. Death has been accepted as a fact. But it is to be vanquished by a miracle of new creation at the last day. Jesus dwells serenely on a spiritual resurrection which takes place through faith in Him. He ignores death altogether. As He speaks, those that are in the tombs hear His voice and come forth.[5] St. Paul seemed to grasp and to build on the mighty thought of the Master, when he declared that believers were risen with Christ, and proceeded to argue that if they were risen with Him they must live a life conformable to the resurrection.

Too readily we take refuge in the heresy that this is a figure of speech. We palm off on our conscience the notion that we can be *more or less* risen with Christ. But the language of Jesus brings us to a stand. Nothing can be more definite than this. Certainly we must, according to His thought, either have heard the voice and come out of the tombs, so that we are now living and living for evermore, or be yet in our sins and therefore dead.

The life of the tombs is painfully real. How well we all know it! The sense of sick corruption within; the haunting memories; the shuddering declensions of the heart; the scornful recognition of our earthy kindred, "I have said to corruption, Thou art my father; to the worm, Thou art my mother and my sister;" the dismal effort to whitewash the

[1] John v. 28.

outside with pleasures and interests, and the affectation of content, because the rank and noisome atmosphere is intolerable.

Equally real and unmistakable is the life of resurrection. When they who are in the tombs come forth there is a complete change. Fragrance breathes through the charmed air; flowers blow; and the time of the singing of birds has come. Righteousness, peace, and joy in the Holy Ghost flood the inward life, like the coming in of the day, and a firm hand lays hold on immortality.

The really pertinent question is therefore that which seems to be presupposed in all these discourses of Jesus, not—What will happen at the last day? Shall you and I wake out of the dust and resume the garments of the flesh? but—Are we risen with Christ now, because according to His own incomparable thought, *I am the Resurrection and the Life; he that believeth on me, though he die, yet shall he live?*

(2) In the same way, here as in the Synoptics, He regards His second coming and the judgment of the world as beginning from His own death and consequent ascent to glory. When He had appealed to heaven, *Father, glorify Thy name*, and for the sake of those that stood by the responsive voice had sounded from heaven, He exclaimed, *Now is the judgment of this world.*[1] And His return in the person of the Paraclete, which filled His thoughts in the farewell discourse, would commence at once a process of judgment.[2] Indeed, as we have already

[1] John xii. 31.   [2] John xvi. 11.

seen, His word, which of course He knew would be preserved by the recording power of the Holy Spirit, would be the abiding judge of men.[1]

It is this unique idea of judgment, as a spiritual process initiated by His incarnation and continued by His Spirit, that explains a paradox, which the evangelist feels to be so completely met by the body of the discourses that he does not hesitate to leave the apparently contradictory statements lying side by side : *The Father hath given all judgment unto the Son;*[2] *He gave Him authority to execute judgment because He is the Son of Man :*[3] and yet, *I judge no man;*[4] *I came not to judge the world but to save the world.*[5]

This of course must mean that Jesus does not judge men, as an earthly judge sits in judgment on his fellows, or as we all so freely pass our opinions upon one another. His purpose in the world is not of this censorious or even judicial character. But, from the moment of His completed work, when His life, His death, His resurrection, and His return through the Spirit were permanently before the world, that was the factor by which every one would be judged, or rather would judge himself. Every one would settle his destiny by determining what he thinks of Christ. " He that believeth on Him is not judged ; he that believeth not hath been judged already, because he hath not believed in the name of the only begotten Son of God. And this is the judgment, that the Light is come into the world."[6]

[1] John xii. 48. [2] John v. 22. [3] John v. 27.
[4] John viii. 15. [5] John xii. 47. [6] John iii. 18, 19.

The historical manifestation of Jesus in its entirety was to constitute, and has constituted, a standard by which men are necessarily tested. Just as in the scenes of the judgment and crucifixion of Jesus, every one concerned in the event seems to be thrown up into a vivid light and judged—Pilate the vacillating and shifty sceptic, the priests with their prodigious religion and godlessness combined, Peter the impetuous and as yet ill-balanced believer, Judas the cankered and avaricious soul, betrayed rather than betraying—so all mankind, as they are brought to the touchstone of Jesus, are revealed and judged. Just what we are, appears by our relation to Him. Some of us see nothing to desire in Him at all— though perhaps only a few. Therein they pronounce a verdict on themselves. Others believe from fear, but are not transformed into His image. By the image of Him in whom we believe we are infallibly judged. Many pass Him by, look Him in the face and pass Him by. There is no hostility, no denial, no doubt. They are simply indifferent. The lusts of other things occupy the soul. The life, the death, the resurrection of Jesus, and His present operation through the Spirit, are of no interest to them. And this—such seems to be the thought of Jesus—virtually judges them. They look the only begotten Son of God in the face; they survey His character; they hear His teaching; they contemplate His sufferings; listlessly they hear that some saw Him risen; but they find no affinity with Him, no personal sympathy or vivid relation. And in this they are judged; judged just as one is judged who glances round the National Gallery and says, "I see no pictures here to admire," or hears the masterpieces of Beethoven and prefers the songs of the music hall.

This of course implies that only they to whom the truth has been presented can be judged by it. Indeed, Jesus Himself declares that His contemporaries would not have had sin if they had not seen and hated Him. It was the presence of the Light which made it an all-involuntary judge of those who loved darkness rather than light. And as we are assured that He came not to judge but to save the world, we may perhaps assume—though Jesus never states it in so many words—that every human soul that ever lived will have the opportunity of believing in Christ—such an opportunity as we have had and have. In fact it seems to follow from the idea of an absolute criterion of human life and conduct, that every human being should be brought into contact with it. And if, from the exigencies of history, this criterion could only come into the region of historical reality late in time, and then could only be made known gradually to the subsequent generations of men, there would necessarily be in the counsels of God some mode of rectifying the accidents of temporal or spatial conditions, by bringing every human being, even after the death of the body, to the definite issue of a choice. Every one will be compelled to say, or to show, what he thinks of Jesus, and by that verdict, self-passed, every one will be judged.

(3) Thus a careful student of His words will observe that Jesus regards heaven and hell as

states of being actually found in this present life. He addresses His blinded and prejudiced opponents as already in hell : *Ye are of your father the devil*, He says, and the lusts of your father it is your will to do.[1] Men already, while they are on the earth, are capable of being born into that diabolical family and household, just as they can be born of God ; and Jesus does not hesitate to assert that certain persons are in that awful situation. Or again, in language the exact force of which is a little lost, because we do not distinguish between the *present* of custom and the *present* of fact, Jesus speaks of those who are not in Him but cast forth as already undergoing the penal fires : *If a man abide not in me, he is cast forth as a branch and is withered, and they gather them and cast them into the fire, and they are burning.*[2] Here He does not seem to be describing in general terms what customarily happens, but rather to be sketching what He observes before His eyes, the boughs wrenched from His vitalising Person, withered, cast into the fire, and perishing in the flames. As Dante was to his generation "the man who had been in hell," Jesus is the one Teacher who in all generations touches this appalling subject with a convincing sincerity ; because, seeing the human heart as it is, He describes the horrors into which it is plunged by sin, and in denunciation of punishment does not refer to what shall be, so much as to what actually is, the verifiable outcome of wrongdoing.

On the other hand, His sketch of " His own " as *in the world but not of the world*, presents all the

[1] John viii. 44.   [2] John xv. 6.

attractive features which are popularly associated with heaven. His joy is theirs; so is His peace; so even is His supernatural power. And though they are on pilgrimage still, not yet having crossed the river, they move through a land of Beulah. To quote the beautiful words of the maiden Polissena, one of "Christ's folk in the Apennines,"[1] they "have two heavens, one here and one beyond." Whatever glories may lie far away in the future, their present state deserves a heavenly designation, for, says Jesus, *the glory which Thou hast given me I have given unto them, that they may be one, even as we are; I in them, and Thou in me, that they may be perfected into one.*[2]

That is certainly a delineation of a completed heaven, to which it does not seem possible to add any essential feature. And when it is further declared that the Father loves them as He loves Jesus, no point can be said to be missing. It is a state on earth, but it is no earthly state. And the great bulk of the last discourse of Jesus remains unintelligible until it is observed that He is laying down the lines of a heavenly life which He intends His disciples to live in Him on this side the grave.

II. But while this present and practical interest is manifest in all that Jesus says about the last things, as if this were indeed the last day in which we are all living, since He came, this does not prevent Him from referring here, quite as distinctly as in the Synoptics, to a consummation in time of the processes which are already in operation.

[1] I refer to Miss Alexander's book of this name published by Mr. Ruskin. [2] John xvii. 22, 23.

1. Quite apart from the present resurrection, which occurs when the soul believes in Him, there is to be, He declares, a general resurrection: *They that have done good shall come forth unto the resurrection of life; and they that have done ill unto the resurrection of judgment.*[1] But evidently He does not regard the "resurrection of judgment" as in the real sense of the term a resurrection at all, for it is only of those who have entered into the relation of faith with Himself that He can speak of being really raised up. *That which He hath given me:*[2] *every one that beholdeth the Son and believeth on Him;*[3] *him that eateth my flesh and drinketh my blood I will raise up at the last day.*[4]

Certainly Jesus permits Himself some obscurity in this matter. For we may ask, if the believer is not to see death, what is meant by *I will raise him up at the last day?* And if all shall rise, what is the meaning of attaching the special promise to believers only? And again, does He mean to convey the idea that between the natural death and that raising up at the last day the soul of the believer shall be unconscious, in the unnoticed sleep of death? It is all left vague and uncertain, as if to impress upon men the necessity of seeking and obtaining their real resurrection now. It is not safe to slip into the drowsy tides of death unless there is already wound about the spirit the infrangible cord of immortality.

2. The picturesque details of the judgment which

---

[1] John v. 29.
[3] John vi. 40.
[2] John vi. 39.
[4] John vi. 54.

are to be found in Matthew and Luke are wholly wanting in John. But the passage already quoted[1] seems to imply that, in addition to the implicit trial by the standard of His incarnation which has been necessarily proceeding ever since He was raised to the right hand of God, there will be also a final assembly of the whole human race before God to receive the deeds done in the body. If Jesus teaches this—though it is by no means an essential part of the idea of final judgment—it is in itself by no means inconceivable. Consider the meaning of the star-dust at one end, and of an ant-hill at the other end, of the scale of the Creation. The mind that maintains those incalculable stellar systems and at the same time animates the million communities of ants, is certainly quite capable of carrying out such an idea. The details may be beyond our imagination, as presumably the marshalled forces of industry and war would be beyond the comprehension of an ant; but the fact is reasonable enough, and does not fail in impressiveness. It is said that the whole present population of the globe could stand in ten square miles of space; and that means that all the tribes of men since the world began could stand in the area of a few English counties. And supposing that time is no more, and the unhasting eternities lie open for that long assize, there is no difficulty in believing—that is, there is no greater miracle involved than that which the existence of a race like our own implies at every turn—that the Maker of men will summon them all

[1] John v. 29.

together before His dread bar, and patiently pass judgment on each through the Man whom He has appointed.

3. But a final thought is brought out in gem-like clearness by these last heart-to-heart utterances of Jesus. It is that He personally will come again. His coming through that other Comforter would not dispense with another entrance into this world of time and space: *If I will that he tarry till I come, what is that to thee?* [1] He asked, though that one did not tarry more than a century, and now eighteen centuries more have passed, and still Jesus has not come again.

Yes, of all the words He uttered, none carry a more unmistakable stamp of His personality, or ring with a more genuine music of conviction, than those in which He declared: *In my Father's house are many mansions; if it were not so I would have told you; for I go to prepare a place for you. And if I go and prepare a place for you, I come again and will receive you unto myself; that where I am there ye may be also.* [2] *Father, that which Thou hast given me, I will that where I am they also may be with me, that they may behold my glory which Thou hast given me.* [3] With our imperfect apprehensions of our present heavenly possession we could hardly, for all the joy and peace of the Christian life, repress some tearful sighs of disappointment if this were all, if the best were not to be. But here is a high and sufficient assurance. The heaven we have is a pledge of the heaven which is to be. Believing in Him, whose teaching has

[1] John xxi. 22.   [2] John xiv. 2-4.   [3] John xvii. 24.

been occupying our minds and stirring our hearts, we assuredly enter into a rest—but a rest remaineth for the people of God. We have tasted a manna sent down from heaven; but the land flowing with milk and honey is yet in reserve. Certain mansions of our Father's house which lie along the line of pilgrimage have been open to us, and we have repeatedly in them been entertained with banquet and with song. But, we surmise, sitting at the feet of Jesus, that the starry heavens, "that wide and shining house of God," are not more vastly removed above the poor littleness of "this dim spot that men call earth," than the range of mansions in the Father's house excels even those fair habitations in which we have sojourned.

INDEX OF REFERENCES TO PASSAGES FROM THE GOSPELS

MATTHEW—	PAGE	MATTHEW—	PAGE
iii. 2	31	xi. 27	24, 46, 158, 172, 194
iv. 17	31		
v. 3–10	33	28	59, 118
17	23	xii. 6	46
20	81	28	35, 114
22	73	29	116
24	89	30	117
45	63, 76	31–33	73, 146
48	83	35	70
vi. 22, 23	69	37	151
26	76	50	61
vii. 11	64, 76	xiii. 11	31
12	91	18	114
15–20	137	41	148
21	61, 151	43	137
23	85, 148	46	99
viii. 12	33	xv. 11	76
ix. 5	110	13	61
35–38	105	17	136
x. 27	136	xvi. 14	14
29, 30	76	16	49, 194
32	61, 151	17	61
40	117	18	125
xi. 5	113	19	131
11	36	26	64, 92
19	76	27	147, 152
22	72	xviii. 3	68, 105
25	116	11	97

… INDEX TO PASSAGES FROM THE GOSPELS

MATTHEW—	PAGE		MARK—	PAGE
xviii. 14	. . . 65		viii. 12	. . 113
17	. . . 125		28	. . . 14
18	. . . 131		30	. . . 49
19	. . . 133		31, 32	. . . 119
20	. . 118, 132		36	. . . 64
22	. . . 91		ix. 42	. . . 106
23	. . . 68		45, 47	. . . 219
35	. . . 68		49	. . . 136
xx. 6	. . . 92		x. 14	. . . 71
16	. . . 103		15	. . 36, 99
25	. . . 134		21	. . . 82
28	. . 120, 135		32	. . . 120
xxi 33	. . . 207		45	. . . 120
43	. . . 33		xi. 18	. . . 155
xxii. 2	. . . 46		27	. . . 76
11	. . . 103		xii. 30, 31	. . . 90
14	. . . 103		xiii. 2, 4, 6	. . . 207
xxiii. 8–10	. . . 134		30	. . . 18
39	. . . 145		xiv. 24	. . . 121
xxiv. 22	. . . 79		xv. 43	. . . 29
24	. . . 104			
34	. 18, 142		LUKE—	
36	. 139, 142		ii. 49	. . . 58
xxv. 31	. 146, 151		iv. 18	. . . 113
34	. . . 37		vii. 47	. . . 108
46	. . . 150		ix. 20	. . . 49
xxvi. 28	. 109, 122		x. 3	. . . 136
64	. . . 145		18, 19	. . . 118
xxviii. 20	. . . 157		20	. . . 104
			28	. . . 82
MARK—			xi. 20	. . . 35
i. 15	. 105, 253		21	. . . 116
27	. 14, 215		29	. . . 114
ii. 17	. . . 102		34–36	. . . 69
iii. 27	. . . 116		42	. . . 89
29	. . . 67		xii. 8	. . . 117
35	. . . 82		23	. . . 144
iv. 10–32	. . . 17		47, 48	. . . 72
11	. . . 31		50	. . . 120
14	. . . 114		51	. . . 136
vii. 18, 19	. . . 136		xiii. 26, 27	. . . 137

INDEX TO PASSAGES FROM THE GOSPELS

LUKE—	PAGE
xiv. 14	91, 147
15	29
16	98
xv. 5	107
7	68, 97
xvi. 9	91
16	37
17	29
xviii. 17	36
18, 24	219
xix. 9	95
10	97
xx. 9	207
35	147
36	107, 147
xxi. 32	18
xxii. 18–20	232
32	105
35–37	136
xxiv. 29	14

JOHN—	PAGE
i. 13	255
18	202
29	245
45	191
ii. 19–22	164, 259
22	165
iii. 3	220
5	262
8	176, 253
11	192
12	231
13, 14	46, 210
15	219, 220, 254
16–21	163, 166, 180, 196, 232
18	254, 274
19	166, 274
iv. 14	222, 227
21–24	261

JOHN—	PAGE
iv. 22	228
24	176
25	191
34	198
36	222
44	192
v. 17	177
18	195
20	196
22	196, 274
23	194
24	222, 230, 271
25	228, 271
26	176, 196, 226
27	46, 192, 274
28	272
29	256, 279, 280
30	197, 200
34	179, 228
38	192
40	179
43	200
44	179
vi. 15	47
27	46, 222
29	192, 257
33	211
37	257
39	279
40	223, 279
45	177, 257
47	223, 254
51	238
53	46
54	223, 279
56	239
57	171, 174
62	46, 210
63	262
68	229
69	191

286 INDEX TO PASSAGES FROM THE GOSPELS

JOHN—	PAGE	JOHN—	PAGE
vii. 16	24, 200	xii. 24	238
17	255	25	222
18	197	31	244, 273
29	192	32, 33	164, 179
37	227	34	193
39	239	46	178, 228
viii. 12	193, 228	47	228, 230, 274
15	274	48	230, 267, 274
28	46	xiii. 1–11	245
29	197	31	46, 201
30	164	34	256
32	229	35	251, 264
35, 36	197	xiv. 1	254
38	210	2–4	281
40	200	6	194, 227
44	182, 277	7	145
46	198	9	194
51	223	10	201
55	197	16	201, 240
58	210	18	240
ix. 2	208	21	240
3	182	25	166
35, 36	201	26	155, 165
x. 9	228	27	263
10	221	30	198, 243, 244
11–18	243, 244	xv. 1	228, 239, 255
16	259	3	113, 230
17	181	6	277
24	191	7	230
27	260	xvi. 1–3	262
28	222	8	265
30	187	10	197, 255
36	192, 196, 199	12	256
xi. 25	194, 267	13	235, 248
26	223, 271	16	240
27	191	18–20	262
41	201	24	263
42	260	26, 27	264
52	259	33	198, 247
xii. 16	165	xvii. 3	167, 192, 226
23	46	5	210

INDEX TO PASSAGES FROM THE GOSPELS

JOHN—	PAGE	JOHN—	PAGE
xvii. 8	. 230	xvii. 22	183, 228, 278
9	. 258	23	. . 278
10	. . 201	24	181, 210, 281
11	. . 273	xviii. 37	. . 230
13	. . . 263	xx. 19	. . . 265
14	. . . 180	23	. . . 265
19	. . 245	24	. . . 265
20, 21	. . . 251, 252, 260, 264	xxi. 22	. . 281
		24	. . 161

The Gospel and the Age Series.

3/6 EACH.   Large Crown 8vo, gilt top.   **3/6** EACH.

1. **THE GOSPEL AND THE AGE.** Sermons on Special Occasions. By the late W. C. MAGEE, D.D., Archbishop of York.

   SPECTATOR :—
   "*Will arrest the attention of the world.*"

   SATURDAY REVIEW :—
   "*It is impossible not to be indebted to a champion who can defend the truth with such intellectual force and such choice incisive language.*"

   RECORD :—
   "*It contains the 'Gospel,' and it preaches to the 'age.' There is in all these sermons the excellence of a giant's strength.*"

   CHURCH BELLS :—
   "*The language is pure, clear, nervous, appropriate, energetic.*"

   METHODIST TIMES :—
   "*Beyond doubt one of the few volumes of sermons worth keeping in constant use as a spiritual and intellectual stimulant.*"

   DUBLIN EXPRESS :—
   "*They must be read and re-read in order that their originality of thought, strength of phrase, and noble orderliness of arrangement may be appreciated.*"

> # The Gospel and the Age Series.

3/6 EACH.   Large Crown 8vo, gilt top.   **3/6** EACH.

2. **GROWTH IN GRACE.** And other Sermons. By the late W. C. MAGEE, D.D., Archbishop of York. With an Introduction by His Grace the Archbishop of Canterbury.

GUARDIAN :—
"*The sermons in this volume show us the Archbishop at his very best.*"

RECORD :—
"*A fit memorial of a preacher of rare eloquence, who did not misuse his magnificent gifts.*"

CHURCH BELLS :—
"*Through every line of them gleams manliness and power.*"

DAILY CHRONICLE :—
"*Pervaded by the remarkable strength and spirituality of the preacher's mind, and addressed with striking force to immediate and practical ends.*"

LITERARY WORLD :—
"*For eloquence and power of sustained thought, these sermons will take rank among the finest pulpit utterances of the day. We can unhesitatingly commend this volume as a great quickener at once of thought and of spiritual life.*"

The Gospel and the Age Series.

3/6 EACH.   Large Crown 8vo, gilt top.   **3/6** EACH.

3. **CHRIST THE LIGHT OF ALL SCRIPTURE.** And other Sermons. By the late W. C. MAGEE, D.D., Archbishop of York.

LITERARY CHURCHMAN :—
"*We give to this volume an unusually earnest recommendation, especially to the clergy. Such sermons as these are invaluable.*"

REVIEW OF THE CHURCHES :—
"*The book is full of a strong, vigorous, and masterful personality. There is much massive thought clearly expressed, much profound and significant reasoning, and an abundance of epigram.*"

GLOBE :—
"*It is hardly necessary to recommend discourses so full of fresh thought and vigorous reflection.*"

LITERARY WORLD :—
"*Marked by the strength of conviction and the eloquent force of language that characterised the author.*"

SCOTSMAN :—
"*The reader will find the generally accepted truths of Christianity set forth with a passionate earnestness, a wealth of illustration, and a power of argument and expression which cannot fail to command his attention and enchain his interest.*"

The Gospel and the Age Series.

3/6   Large Crown 8vo, gilt top.   **3/6**

EACH.   EACH.

4. **THE INDWELLING CHRIST.** And other Sermons. By the late HENRY ALLON, D.D., Minister of Union Chapel, Islington.

    DAILY TELEGRAPH :—
        "*Worthy to take their place among the masterpieces of the old divines .... an enduring testimony to the greatness of a departed preacher.*"

    CHRISTIAN WORLD :—
        "*A book which altogether is worthy to be called a great religious testimony.*"

    BRITISH WEEKLY :—
        "*The final fruits of matured and ripened powers.*"

    LEEDS MERCURY :—
        "*We are thankful that Dr. Allon's strong and tender ministry will still continue in this wise and helpful book.*"

    SUNDAY SCHOOL CHRONICLE :—
        "*Altogether this volume will enhance Dr. Allon's reputation as a great teacher and great spiritual guide.*"

    INDEPENDENT :—
        "*Word and thought are equally characteristic, and together mirror the ripe culture of the preacher's latest years.*"

The Gospel and the Age Series.

3/6 EACH. Large Crown 8vo, gilt top. **3/6** EACH.

5. **CHRIST AND SOCIETY.** And other Sermons. By DONALD MACLEOD, D.D., one of H.M. Chaplains.

SCOTSMAN :—
  "*Admirable and seasonable discourses.*"

ROCK :—
  "*Will do much to advance the consideration of great social questions on right lines.*"

GLASGOW HERALD :—
  "*Very remarkable sermons they are.*"

RECORD :—
  "*Fitted to supply a want of the age.*"

DUNDEE COURIER :—
  "*Reverent without being conventional, and eloquent without being unrestrained.*"

EXPOSITORY TIMES :—
  "*Though the treatment is designedly popular, there is plenty of first-hand knowledge displayed. There is also plenty of enthusiasm, plenty of courage, and plenty of assurance.*"

METHODIST TIMES :—
  "*Business men will do well to add this volume to their library.*"

The Gospel and the Age Series.

3/6 EACH.   Large Crown 8vo, gilt top.   **3/6** EACH.

6. **THE CHRISTIAN CERTAINTIES.** Discourses in Exposition and Defence of the Christian Faith. By JOHN CLIFFORD, M.A., D.D.

QUIVER:—

> "*Eloquent and incisive as these teachings are, they come as a valuable addition to the armoury of those who are fighting for the faith in an age when all men are asking first and foremost for certainty.*"

STAR:—

> "*On the ethical and social aspects of religion Dr. Clifford speaks with great freshness and impressiveness.*"

CHRISTIAN WORLD:—

> "*This book contains some of the brightest utterances on vital religious questions in the range of English contemporary theology.*"

WESTMINSTER REVIEW:—

> "*Vigorous and eloquent.*"

PALL MALL GAZETTE:—

> "*The book is a suggestive one, and will be read with keen interest.*"

The Gospel and the Age Series.

3/6 EACH.   Large Crown 8vo, gilt top.   **3/6** EACH.

7. **CHRIST AND ECONOMICS.** In the Light of the Sermon on the Mount. By the Very Rev. C. W. STUBBS, D.D., Dean of Ely.

ECONOMICAL REVIEW :—

"*Plain, sensible, manly Christian teaching on the duties of citizenship, the evils of vulgar luxury, the proper use of wealth, and kindred topics. It is truly refreshing to find that there lives so faithful and worthy a disciple of Maurice and Kingsley—both in theology and social teaching.*"

INQUIRER :—

"*Full of the social teachings which the age most requires . . . . interesting and instructive from beginning to end.*"

ECHO :—

"*Full of the Christianity of Christ.*"

LEEDS MERCURY :—

"*The book is thought-compelling, and the stamp of broad but uncompromising patriotism is upon its eloquent pages.*"

CHRISTIAN LEADER :—

"*Full of knowledge, of courage, and of hope.*"

The Gospel and the Age Series.

3/6 EACH. Large Crown 8vo, gilt top. **3/6** EACH.

8. **CHRIST AND OUR TIMES.** By the Ven. W. MacDonald Sinclair, D.D., Archdeacon of London, Canon of St. Paul's, Chaplain to H.M. the Queen.

ROCK :—
  "*We hope that these valuable discourses, which must have already, as spoken, been a blessing to many, may now, in their more permanent form of print, become a cherished possession in thousands of English homes.*"

SPEAKER :—
  "*A brave and opportune book, which grapples in an honest and open fashion with many of the spiritual difficulties and social problems of the age.*"

QUARTERLY REVIEW :—
  "*Very able and interesting sermons.*"

PALL MALL GAZETTE :—
  "*Many of the questions which agitate or interest men's minds are discussed soberly and effectively in language studiedly calm and unimpassioned, but in words which will satisfy and even charm many a restless inquirer.*"

SUNDAY SCHOOL CHRONICLE :—
  "*Very admirable sermons.*"

The Gospel and the Age Series.

3/6 EACH. Large Crown 8vo, gilt top. **3/6** EACH.

---

9. **THE LORD'S PRAYER.** Sermons preached in Westminster Abbey. By the Very Rev. F. W. FARRAR, D.D., Dean of Canterbury.

RECORD:—

"*Intensely practical. . . . . They call with no uncertain voice to the careless and the impenitent; they touch the everyday life of the hearers.*"

REVIEW OF THE CHURCHES:—

"*The Lord's Prayer has rarely, if ever, received so thorough and sympathetic an exposition, so scholarly and yet so practical. For the preacher this is, in our opinion, the first book on the subject.*"

EXPOSITORY TIMES:—

"*These sermons are less an exposition than an illustration of the Lord's Prayer. And it is an illustration we are most in need of—an illustration as pointed, and rich, and fertile as this.*"

DUNDEE COURIER:—

"*Their wealth of spiritual insight, their calm and exhaustive analysis, their simplicity, their literary finish, will make them to be prized by all.*"

SUNDAY SCHOOL TIMES:—

"*Sure of a wide reading.*"

The Gospel and the Age Series.

3/6 EACH.   Large Crown 8vo, gilt top.   **3/6** EACH.

10. **THE COMRADE-CHRIST.** And other Sermons. By the Rev. W. J. DAWSON, Author of "Makers of Modern English," &c.

SCOTSMAN:—
"*All display originality of thought, simplicity of style, and vigour of treatment; the volume is sure of a welcome.*"

EXPOSITORY TIMES:—
"*Mr. Dawson's fertility in rapid, telling phrase — phrase that tells upon the ears of hurrying passers-by— is matchless.*"

MANCHESTER GUARDIAN:—
"*There is a real freshness and force of thought which lifts these sermons above the level of the conventional.*"

METHODIST TIMES:—
"*Fresh and poetic in conception, vigorous in utterance, and ever up-to-date; living sermons for a living age.*"

GREAT THOUGHTS:—
"*They deserve a place in every library. His words are winged, and full of life and energy. Vigorous, incisive, trenchant, they are often, as Julius Hare said of Luther's—'half-battles.'*"

CHRISTIAN WORLD:—
"*Fully maintains the high level of pulpit work shown in his previously published discourses.*"

The Gospel and the Age Series.

3/6 EACH.   Large Crown 8vo, gilt top.   **3/6** EACH.

11. **CHRIST AND SCEPTICISM.** And other Sermons. By the Rev. S. A. ALEXANDER, M.A., Reader of the Temple Church, London.

RECORD:—

"*Valuable contributions to the available defences of Christianity along its moral, historical, rational, and spiritual lines.*"

QUIVER:—

"*So high and strong in tone that all who are labouring in the field of Christian evidences owe to its author a deep debt of gratitude.*"

MANCHESTER GUARDIAN:—

"*Clear in style, and, without parade, show wide reading, and a mind thoughtful and earnest.*"

CHRISTIAN WORLD:—

"*An admirable volume of virile addresses.*"

SCOTSMAN:—

"*The book, which shows large acquaintance with the subject discussed, and is written in a calm, judicial, and sympathetic spirit, may be commended to religious inquirers who are repelled by narrow-minded dogmatism.*"

The Gospel and the Age Series.

3/6 EACH.   Large Crown 8vo, gilt top.   **3/6** EACH.

12. **LABOUR AND SORROW.** Sermons on various occasions. By the Rev. W. J. KNOX LITTLE, M.A., Canon of Worcester Cathedral.

CHURCH REVIEW :—
   "This striking and powerful book contains within its pages much Christian philosophy, powerful rhetoric, and deeply emotional writing."

GREAT THOUGHTS :—
   "A volume of brilliant sermons."

ECCLESIASTICAL GAZETTE :—
   "We think this volume equal to any that has come from the writer's pen, and we wish it a wide circulation."

INQUIRER :—
   "In these Sermons there is a precious mine of reading for every devout man and woman."

LONDON QUARTERLY REVIEW :—
   "Suggestive and helpful, the outcome of much study of human nature, and God's ways of perfecting it."

The Gospel and the Age Series.

3/6 EACH. Large Crown 8vo, gilt top. **3/6** EACH.

13. **ESSENTIAL CHRISTIANITY.** A Series of Explanatory Sermons. By the Rev. HUGH PRICE HUGHES, M.A.

THE NEW AGE:—

"*Preachers who wish to speak a living message to living men will do well to possess and ponder this vigorous volume.*"

PRESBYTERIAN:—

"*The ground it covers, and the freshness of thought which pervades it, will be found to make it both instructive and stimulating to every Christian preacher and teacher.*"

SCOTSMAN:—

"*Mr. Hughes puts life and originality into his sermons.*"

SUNDAY SCHOOL CHRONICLE:—

"*An excellent book to put into the hands of young men who may be in danger of being drawn away into the dreary regions of unbelief.*"

LONDON QUARTERLY REVIEW:—

"*Full of ardent evangelical zeal.*"

The Gospel and the Age Series.

3/6   Large Crown 8vo, gilt top.   3/6

EACH.   EACH.

14. **VOICES AND SILENCES.** By the Very Rev. H. D. M. SPENCE, D.D., Dean of Gloucester.

GUARDIAN:—

"*A preacher who really studies such a volume as this will find that he has added very much to the solid matter which must provide the backbone of every sermon.*"

ROCK:—

"*The book covers pretty well the entire range of Church work, and is one which every one who takes up will read with pleasure.*"

MANCHESTER GUARDIAN:—

"*Earnest and interesting.*"

REVIEW OF THE CHURCHES:—

"*It has many excellent qualities — is devout, touched with emotion, and full of the most passionate loyalty to Christ.*"

METHODIST TIMES:—

"*Its practical homilies have a message for the times.*"

The Gospel and the Age Series.

3/6 EACH.   Large Crown 8vo, gilt top.   **3/6** EACH.

15. TEN-MINUTE SERMONS. By the Rev. W. ROBERTSON NICOLL, M.A., LL.D., Editor of "The Expositor's Bible," &c.

CHRISTIAN WORLD:—
"*A book to be commended to all Christian people. A book for weary spirits, for distracted and unsettled minds, for hearts world-worn and sorrow-laden, of every calling and sphere in life.*"

GLASGOW HERALD:—
"*Each one of them is a thoughtful, polished essay, as lofty in tone as it is straightforward and vigorous in expression.*"

INDEPENDENT:—
"*What strikes us very much in these brief sermons is the union of intellectual power with deep spiritual feeling.*"

LITERARY WORLD:—
"*It is a beautiful book, strong because so calm, suggestive, and only not eloquent because no room is found in it for mere rhetoric.*"

LONDON QUARTERLY:—
"*It will profit busy men who have leisure enough to digest as well as to read; and it will set preachers thinking.*"

The Gospel and the Age Series.

3/6 Large Crown 8vo, gilt top. **3/6**
EACH. EACH.

New Volumes.

16. **TEMPTATION AND TOIL.** By the Rev. W. HAY M. H. AITKEN, M.A., Author of "The Love of the Father," &c.

17. **THE TEACHING OF JESUS.** By R. F. HORTON, M.A., D.D., Author of "Revelation and the Bible," &c.

18. **THE KNOWLEDGE OF GOD.** And other Sermons. By J. H. BERNARD, D.D., Fellow of Trinity College, Dublin.

Other Volumes in Preparation.

ISBISTER & CO., LIMITED,
COVENT GARDEN, LONDON, W.C.

www.ingramcontent.com/pod-product-compliance
Lightning Source LLC
Chambersburg PA
CBHW032044230426
43672CB00009B/1466